MORE FOUL DEEDS & SUSPICIOUS DEATHS IN AND AROUND CHESTERFIELD

FOUL DEEDS AND SUSPICIOUS DEATHS Series

Foul Deeds and Suspicious Deaths series explores in detail crimes of passion, brutal murders, grisly deeds and foul misdemeanours. From Victorian street crime, to more modern murder where passion, jealousy, or social deprivation brought unexpected violence to those involved. From mysterious death to murder and manslaughter, the books are a fascinating insight into not only those whose lives are forever captured by the suffering they endured, but also into the society that moulded and shaped their lives. Each book takes you on a journey into the darker and unknown side of the area.

Other titles in the series

Foul Deeds and Suspicious Deaths in Blackburn & Hyndburn, Steve Greenhalgh
ISBN: 1-903425-18-2
160pp . Illustrated. £9.99

Foul Deeds and Suspicious Deaths in and around Chesterfield, Geoffrey Sadler
ISBN: 1-903425-30-1
160pp . Illustrated . £9.99

Foul Deeds and Suspicious Deaths in & around Durham, Maureen Anderson
ISBN: 1-903425-46-8
176pp . Illustrated . £9.99

Foul Deeds and Suspicious Deaths in and around Halifax, Stephen Wade
ISBN: 1-903425-45-X
176pp . Illustrated . £9.99

Foul Deeds and Suspicious Deaths in Leeds, David Goodman
ISBN: 1-903425-08-5
176pp . Illustrated . £9.99

Foul Deeds and Suspicious Deaths in Newcastle, Maureen Anderson
ISBN: 1-903425-34-4
176pp. Illustrated £ 9.99

Foul Deeds and Suspicious Deaths in Nottingham, Kevin Turton
ISBN: 1-903425-35-2
176pp . Illustrated . £9.99

Foul Deeds and Suspicious Deaths around Pontefract and Castleford, Keith Henson
ISBN: 1-903425-54-9
176pp. Illustrated £ 9.99

Foul Deeds and Suspicious Deaths in and around Rotherham, Kevin Turton
ISBN: 1-903425-27-1
160pp . Illustrated . £9.99

Foul Deeds and Suspicious Deaths Around the Tees, Maureen Anderson
ISBN: 1-903425-26-3
176pp . Illustrated . £9.99

More Foul Deeds and Suspicious Deaths in Wakefield, Kate Taylor
ISBN: 1-903425-48-4
176pp. Illustrated £9.99

Foul Deeds and Suspicious Deaths in York, Keith Henson
ISBN: 1-903425-33-6
176pp . Illustrated . £9.99

Foul Deeds and Suspicious Deaths on the Yorkshire Coast, Alan Whitworth
ISBN: 1-903425-01-8
192pp . Illustrated . £9.99

Please contact us via any of the methods below for more information or a catalogue.
WHARNCLIFFE BOOKS
47 Church Street – Barnsley – South Yorkshire – S70 2AS
Tel: 01226 734555 – 734222 Fax: 01226 734438
E-mail: enquiries@pen-and-sword.co.uk – Website: www.wharncliffebooks.co.uk

More Foul Deeds & Suspicious Deaths in and around
CHESTERFIELD

GEOFFREY SADLER

Series Editor
Brian Elliott

Wharncliffe Books

First Published in Great Britain in 2004 by
Wharncliffe Local History
an imprint of
Pen and Sword Books Ltd.
47 Church Street
Barnsley
South Yorkshire
S70 2AS

Copyright © Geoffrey Sadler, 2004

ISBN: 1-903425-68-9

The right of Geoffrey Sadler to be identified as Author of
this Work has been asserted by him in accordance with the
Copyright, Designs and Patents Act 1988.

A CIP catalogue record for this book is available from the
British Library.

Typeset in 11/13pt Plantin by Mac Style Ltd, Scarborough.

Printed and bound in England by
CPI UK.

Pen and Sword Books Ltd incorporates the Imprints of
Pen & Sword Aviation, Pen & Sword Maritime,
Pen & Sword Military, Wharncliffe Local History,
Pen & Sword Select, Pen and Sword Military Classica
and Leo Cooper.

For a complete list of Pen & Sword titles please contact
PEN & SWORD BOOKS LIMITED
47 Church Street
Barnsley
South Yorkshire
S70 2BR
England
E-mail: enquiries@pen-and-sword.co.uk
Website: www.pen-and-sword.co.uk

Contents

Introduction

s Derbyshire's second town, and the largest in the
north of the county, Chesterfield with its scenic
location close to the Peak District has proved a
regular attraction for tourists and visitors from all over the
world. Nowadays the town and its surroundings are sought
after as a desirable residential area by newcomers from
elsewhere in Britain, and beyond. This, though, has not always
been the case. Like most other towns of its size and
population, Chesterfield has had its share of violence through
the ages. The first volume of this series, *Foul Deeds &
Suspicious Deaths in and Around Chesterfield*, traced the early
history of murder, violent crime and suicide in Chesterfield
and North Derbyshire from the parish church killings in 1434
to the Victorian town's notorious 'kicking case' of 1882. Sadly
for us all, such murderous urges did not die out with that
bygone age, and homicidal violence – in Derbyshire as
elsewhere – has continued all too obviously into our own time.

More Foul Deeds & Suspicious Deaths takes up the
bloodstained baton in the year of 1882 with a rural shotgun
killing, and continues through to our own day with the horrific
Pottery Cottage massacre of 1977. It explores the darker side
of Chesterfield and its outlying areas, shedding light on a
catalogue of crimes, some of them relatively little known,
others still claiming media attention.

For the last nineteen years I have had the great good fortune
to work in the Chesterfield Local Studies Library, whose
considerable resources have provided me with the basic tools
for my research. Of particular value have been the microfilm
files of the *Derbyshire Times* and *Derbyshire Courier*, both
Chesterfield-based newspapers and often local rivals. In their
pages full accounts are found of most of the crimes detailed
here, together with the police investigations, trials, convictions
or acquittals of the defendants. The Victorian age also saw the
arrival of the coroner's inquest and the beginnings of modern
forensic medicine, both of which were to become increasingly

significant during the twentieth century as providers of evidence as to the cause of death, and often as the means of identifying the murderer.

Careful reading of these reports reveals a variety of motives and methods behind some often shocking crimes. The drink-fuelled family squabble that was to end in 'brotherly murder' at the mining village of Pilsley in 1882, the lure of easy money that prompted the callous robbery and drowning of Cutthorpe farmer Herbert Crookes in the Chesterfield Canal by unknown assailants, the desperate poverty that resulted in parents poisoning their own children for insurance money, and the terrible stigma of debt that led once again to family massacre in the 1900s. Perhaps most shocking and violent of all, the savagery of forbidden or thwarted love, as with the vicious Brackenfield billhook killing, or the axe murder on Highfield Road. The fearful trail leads us on through grim Victorian and Edwardian domestic batterings and razor murders, to the shootings at Wateringbury Grove, Staveley, and Pleasley Vale's Littlewood Farm in the1920s. Closer to home, and within living memory of most, we examine the 'Bubble Car' killings of the 1960s, the still unsolved murders of Barbara Mayo, Teresa Bailey and Mavis Hudson, and the Pottery Cottage killings at Eastmoor. For all of these, the bulk of my findings have been culled from the press reports of the time.

Further useful facts have been obtained from the substantial file of cuttings from the *Sheffield Star* held by the library, from various volumes of T P Wood's *Almanac*, from John Eddleston's excellent book *Murderous Derbyshire*, and *Reflections* magazine. Verbal information from relatives of some of those involved in certain cases has also proved of value.

I would like to express my thanks to my colleagues in the Chesterfield Local Studies Library and County Local Studies Library, Matlock, to Derbyshire Library Service for use of their images, to Philip Cousins for the kind loan of information regarding the Herbert Crookes case, and to the Ordnance Survey for permission to reproduce Old County Series maps. Special thanks must go to my friends Ann Krawszik, and Dennis Middleton, both of whom have toured

North Derbyshire in order to take the excellent photographs shown in the text, and to Alun Waterhouse whose assistance in the field of computer technology has, as ever, been crucial. Finally my thanks go to Brian Elliott and Wharncliffe Books for their kind invitation to continue this interesting project, and for their help and advice in bringing it about.

CHAPTER 1

Brotherly Murder
1882

Guns always lay ready to hand in the homes of the Wray brothers. Thomas, George and Leonard were well known in their native village of Pilsley, both for their close comradeship and their ferocious temper when crossed. Pilsley, which lies a few miles south of Chesterfield and not far from the mining village of Clay Cross, was one of several farming settlements abruptly industrialized by the sinking of coal-mines across North Derbyshire in the early and mid-nineteenth century, and the brothers all worked as colliers at the neighbouring Morton pit. It seems that they were equally active 'after hours' as poachers in the outlying woods and fields, and the shotguns they kept were frequently in use. Basically good-natured, but hard-drinking and often aggressive, the brothers had quarrelled violently on several previous occasions, only to make up and become bosom friends afterwards. Sadly for them, the combination of drink, hot tempers, and loaded weapons, was to prove a combustible and fatal mixture.

On the afternoon of Friday 11 August, Leonard and George Wray left work at the Morton colliery and joined their elder

Morton Road, Pilsley. On the right is the Gladstone Arms, *where the Wray brothers drank before returning home in 1882.* Ann Krawszik

Station Road, Pilsley, showing school on right. In 1882 the mining village of Pilsley saw a drunken quarrel end in a shotgun slaying. Ann Krawszik

brother Thomas for a drink at the *Gladstone Arms* beerhouse. Here the brothers consumed five quarts of beer between them before leaving. They may have gone on to another public house, the *Commercial*, before finally returning home. Once back at his house, Leonard Wray was seen to kick over a bucket outside before entering, and shortly afterwards his wife was heard to scream. Apparently Leonard had picked a quarrel with her about the cooking of his dinner, and had struck her.

Thomas Wray, who was halfway through stripping off his pit clothes in his own house, came out to see his sister-in-law run out into the yard with her husband in hot pursuit. He called out for Leonard to stop, telling his brother he was 'no man, to hit a woman like that'. Leonard angrily told him to mind his own business, and George, also appearing on the scene, warned Thomas that if he tried to interfere between husband and wife, George would fight him. Thomas, equally fired up, needed no further invitation, and he and George grappled together, falling to the ground and scuffling furiously. Forgetting his own quarrel, Leonard, who had started the whole thing, now tried vainly to part his battling siblings. Thomas and George got up and fought on across the yard to its far side, when Thomas broke away and ran back inside his house.

Leonard, realising his brother had gone to find his gun, started to run away, shouting to George to do the same. The latter refused, telling Leonard he was not going to move. It was a fatal attack of Dutch courage, for Thomas now emerged from his house carrying a double-barrelled shotgun, which he fired as he ran forward. He was barely two yards from his target as the weapon was discharged, and George collapsed on the ground. He had taken the full impact of the blast in his leg, and now blood poured from the wound as he struggled to get up. Leonard, who had been in full flight over the nearby railway bridge, heard the noise of the shot and turned hurriedly back, only to find Thomas standing over his fallen brother and holding the smoking shotgun. Leonard snatched the weapon from his elder brother's hands, and saw that one of the barrels had been fired. Thomas, still in the grip of his murderous rage, went running back to the house, where he kept another, single-barrelled gun. Leonard fired off the second barrel of the weapon he held, rendering it harmless, and chased after his fleeing brother. Luckily he managed to seize the single-barrelled gun, and discharged it into the wall of the house before Thomas could make use of it.

The brothers came back to find George lying in a pool of blood by the pigsty. Seeing Thomas, the stricken man said: 'Oh Tom, you have killed me', and to Leonard: 'Len, my son, I am a dead man.' Neighbours who had witnessed the shooting went to find a doctor and a policeman, and the local constable P C Rowland arrived on the scene at 6 pm, to find George still lying in the yard with his leg bleeding badly. He informed the policeman: 'I'm done this time, I am shot', and Thomas, still glaring down at him, told the constable: 'I shot him.' A few moments afterwards the rage appeared to leave him, and he remarked: 'Poor George, I don't know why I did it.'

By now, it was too late for remorse. Rowland and others helped him get his clothes back on, and he was cautioned. Meanwhile Mr Lloyd, assistant to Dr Stamford of Tibshelf, attended to give medical help. Seeing the bad state of the wound, Lloyd bound it up as best he could, and confirmed with George's mother that she wished him to be taken to the Chesterfield Hospital. A horse and trap had been brought up, but Lloyd refused to let George travel in it, instead sending for an ambulance cart as a more suitable means of transport. George Kidger, another witness, stayed with Thomas while

Rowland and others helped get the injured man to the hospital. George Wray was admitted to the Chesterfield Hospital at 9.45 pm on Friday evening, where he was examined by house surgeon Dr John Rose. On having him removed from the blood-stained ambulance, Rose found that his patient had sustained a bad gunshot wound in the left leg, which had shattered both bones below the knee. The huge, gaping wound was big enough for Rose to place both his fists inside it, and the severe loss of blood had left the victim pale and barely with any pulse at all. After a rapid consultation with the medical staff, it was decided that the only chance was to amputate the leg from immediately above the knee. The operation was carried out by Dr John Carnegie, the patient having been mercifully given an anaesthetic. The amputation was successful, but by this time George Wray was too far gone to recover. He died at 11.10 pm from shock and loss of blood. He was thirty-nine years old.

His elder brother Thomas had already been taken into custody. He appeared at the Coroner's Inquest, which was held on the following Monday at the Chesterfield Hospital, his

A terraced row in the neighbouring village of Morton, another former mining settlement, where the Wray brothers worked at the local colliery. Dennis Middleton

bandaged head indicating that he bore minor scars of his own. Leonard Wray took the stand as a witness, and while giving an accurate version of events lodged a plea on his brother's behalf. According to him, Thomas didn't know what he was doing when he carried out the murderous attack. Apparently the eldest of the Wrays had suffered two separate head injuries while working in the pit in past years, and after the second of these Leonard claimed that: 'he has at times seemed very queer, especially when he has had drink'. Possibly this might explain the violent assault that Thomas had made two years ago on a gamekeeper at Hardstoft, for which he had been jailed for three months. Few of those listening at the inquest would have needed much convincing of Leonard's comment on his brother that 'when he gets into a passion, he is fearful'. On the other hand, there seemed to be some truth in his claim that Thomas was carrying the shotgun low, its barrels pointing downward, when the weapon was fired. This was probably the reason that George Wray was struck in the leg, rather than the chest or stomach, where a deliberate killing shot would have been aimed. It did not cut much ice with the jury, who having heard the evidence of several other eye-witnesses, returned a verdict of wilful murder. More than that, they registered their disapproval of some of the witnesses, who they felt had given their evidence 'in a very reluctant manner.' The Coroner expressed his agreement with this statement. One suspects that the censured witnesses, most of them neighbours of the brothers, regarded Thomas Wray as not responsible for his actions, and were not eager to help him to the gallows.

Thomas Wray appeared at the Winter Assizes in Derby on Tuesday 31 October 1882, to face the charge of murdering his brother. Once again the evidence was heard, and this time found a more sympathetic hearing. The decision of the jury, deferred until two days later, was one of manslaughter, with a recommendation for mercy. On Friday 3 November, Wray was sentenced to ten years' imprisonment. In the days that followed, he no doubt had time to reflect on how a few moments of uncontrollable, drink-fuelled rage had cost the life of his beloved brother, and taken away a decade of his own.

CHAPTER 2

He was Pleasant and Agreeable
1883

The two well-dressed gentlemen who called at The Cottage and arranged to take a room there seemed to be eminently suitable, and Mrs Marchant, who kept the house for guests with her husband George, was only too happy to admit them. The 'elderly gentleman' who acted as the spokesman, and his younger companion, were both evidently well-to-do and well-spoken, with impeccable manners, and she was later to recall of the younger gentleman that 'he was pleasant and agreeable – you could not wish for a nicer person.' The fact that they insisted on keeping their identities secret and refused to sign the visitor's book, was a

John Smedley's Hydropathic Establishment, Bank Road, Matlock, now Derbyshire County Hall. Smedley put Matlock on the map as a Victorian spa town, probably one reason for the fatal visit of Rev Julius Benn and his son in 1883. Dennis Middleton

little unusual, to be sure, but no doubt they had their reasons. From what she was able to make out, they were here on account of the young man's health – the older man, who referred to the younger one as 'Willie', told her 'my son has been unwell, but he is better now' – and throughout their stay she noticed that he was most attentive and solicitous to the welfare of his companion.

There was nothing remarkable in that, of course. Set in the Peak District twelve miles south-west of Chesterfield, Matlock offered spectacular views and places of interest, and had long been known as a spa town. Since John Smedley had set up his Hydropathic Establishment halfway up the steep hillside approached by Bank Road, visitors had flocked to the town to 'take the waters' and improve their health at this, Derbyshire's answer to Bath. Mrs Marchant's cottage was at the top of the hill on Chesterfield Road, in the area known as Matlock Bridge, and was well situated for explorations of the landmarks around the town. From the time they arrived, on Tuesday 27 February 1883, the two visitors made a thorough investigation of their surroundings. Over the next few days they ventured out to Buxton, walking back as far as Miller's Dale, and to Cromford. Around Matlock itself they explored the caverns and viewed the eighteenth century folly known as Riber Castle, and climbed the Heights of Abraham at Matlock Bath. Both men told her how much they had enjoyed their stay, but kept up their secretive habits, and at their request no-one was allowed to visit them in their upstairs room. As neither of them had thus far given her any cause for alarm, Mrs Marchant did not object.

On Sunday morning, about 7 am, as Mrs Marchant was getting dressed, she heard a bumping or knocking noise which she presumed was the sound of her mother rapping for attention in the room below, but when she asked what was the matter the old lady denied having knocked for her. Thinking no more about it, Mrs Marchant prepared boiled eggs for her guests' breakfast, but the two gentlemen did not appear at the given time. This was unusual, for they were normally very punctual. The Marchants consumed the eggs themselves, and prepared two more in readiness for the two men. Still they did not appear, and at 9 am Mrs Marchant went upstairs and tapped on the door. The only response she got was a muffled sound which she interpreted as acknowledgement that the older gentleman heard her, but did not wish to wake the younger man. Listening from her own bedroom, she heard snoring which indicated her younger guest was still asleep. During the morning, while Mr Marchant was at the chapel service, she made several visits upstairs, only to be met with the same muttered reply as before. By 1 pm, when her husband returned home, Mrs Marchant was extremely worried, thinking that one of her guests must be unwell. At her insistence, and himself sensing that something must be wrong, Mr Marchant went upstairs and knocked on the door. It was promptly unbolted from inside.

At once he was subjected to a horrifying vision. The young man, who had evidently opened the door, stood silent in front of him. He was bleeding badly from a gash in his throat, and his nightshirt, beard, hands, feet and legs were dripping with blood. Still not speaking, he pointed towards the bed, and there lay the older gentleman, himself splashed with blood and with his head smashed in. Shocked and frightened by the horrible sight, Mr Marchant hurriedly escorted his wife and mother out of the house, afraid that they too might be attacked.

Police and medical authorities were called, and Dr Moxon re-entered the cottage with his assistant Mr Hunter and Police Constable Smith. The young man upstairs made no resistance. They discovered that he had attempted to cut his own throat, and was already weak from loss of blood. The constable held him quiet while the medical men stitched up the still bleeding wound. Examination of the older man showed that he was already dead, his face, head and neck battered to a bloody, unrecognisable mass, the brain protruding from the shattered skull. The room itself was a shambles, the floor drenched with blood, while blood-sprays had spattered walls, ceiling, wash-stand, looking-glass and pictures hanging on the walls. The murder weapon was a heavy chamber pot which the younger man had used to batter his companion to death. Afterwards it appeared that he had used a pocket-knife, now bloodstained, in a vain effort to cut his own throat.

Chesterfield Road, Matlock Bridge, where the Benns stayed overnight at the Marchants' guest house prior to the father's murder. Dennis Middleton

Sergeant Gee, who had now arrived on the scene, informed the young man he was under arrest for murder, and took him into custody, where he confessed to having killed his father. He was later removed to the Derby Infirmary. Searching through correspondence received by the dead man, the police were now able to confirm his identity and that of his killer. The victim was the Reverend Julius Benn, a clergyman from Stepney Green in London, where for fifteen years he had been the pastor of the Old Gravel Lane Congregational Meeting House. The young man who had so savagely killed him was his son, William Rutherford Benn, a shipping house clerk. Married only shortly before, in December, to a young lady named Florence Nicholson, he had for some time been suffering from mental problems. He had previously been confined in an asylum following a nervous breakdown, but was released after seeming to recover. His father had brought him to Matlock in the hope that the recovery might be continued, and Sunday's tragedy had been the result.

The Coroner having been consulted, a postmortem was deemed necessary. The inquest took place on Monday and Tuesday, where the cause of death was clearly established as three violent blows to the right side of the head with the chamber pot, which had smashed bones in the skull, destroyed the right ear, and cut through part of the brain. Mr J W Benn, eldest son of the dead man, objected to the post-mortem being carried out, as he felt the cause of death was obvious and there was no need to further 'mutilate' the corpse, but he was assured that the procedure must be followed. It took place in another room. His insistence that the jury take into account the state of the killer's mind was also rejected, the Coroner indicating that this was the business of another jury. The verdict from the inquest was that William Benn should appear at the Assizes on a charge of wilful murder.

On Tuesday 27 March, a month after his arrival at Matlock, William Rutherford Benn was brought before the Hon W M Jervis at the Chief Constable's office on St Mary's Gate in Derby. By this time he was recovered from his self-inflicted injuries, but his mental state still gave cause for concern. He had made a further attempt to kill himself, and had only just been prevented from hurling himself out of a window while at the Derby Infirmary. As a result he was being 'very vigilantly guarded'. Benn was accompanied by the Derby house surgeon, Mr W Benthall, and was handed over to the prison authorities to be confined until his appointment at the forthcoming Assizes.

The Assizes were held soon afterwards, on Wednesday 18 April, but William Rutherford Benn did not appear there; nor was he to stand trial at the Assizes that followed on 28 August. It would seem that, in view of his disturbed mental condition, he was judged unfit to plead; the indications are that his influential relatives may have intervened to have him released, accepting responsibility for his care. Whatever the truth of this, we do know that William returned to his wife, and that the couple had a daughter. This brief domestic idyll ended when Florence Benn died and, as William suffered a relapse their child was brought up by an aunt. The girl was later to achieve lasting fame as the great character actress Margaret Rutherford. She was also to have another famous relation in the world of politics, as William Benn's brother John (the Mr J W Benn of the inquest) had a son and grandson of his own. The latter was, and is, Mr Anthony Wedgwood Benn, who as Tony Benn, MP, until recently represented the town of Chesterfield, only a few miles from the scene of his great-grandfather's murder.

CHAPTER 3

A Watery Grave
1886

Herbert Crookes was a prosperous man of business. The son of an old Cutthorpe farming family, he had previously lived on Glumangate at Chesterfield, where he had been a well-known and popular local tradesman. Now, at thirty-nine, he lived with his wife and five children at Rosene House Farm, in Cutthorpe, and also operated a butcher's business. Two years earlier he had run into financial difficulties through his ownership of a loss-making coal-pit, and had to file for bankruptcy, but those days were now behind him. Herbert was now in a position to expand and acquire more property. For the past year he had owned a butcher's shop in the village of Clowne, and had recently purchased a house there, which he intended to be the new

Sitwell Arms, *Renishaw, one of several stopping-places by farmer Herbert Crookes on his way home from Sheffield to Cutthorpe.* Dennis Middleton

Crown Inn, *Clowne, where Crookes also called on his fateful journey south.* Dennis Middleton

family home. He also had plans to look over premises at Killamarsh, to be set up as a butcher's shop for his son.

On the morning of Wednesday 24 March 1886 Herbert Crookes set off from Rosene House Farm on another business trip. As was his custom, he carried a large amount of money in his pockets, and before leaving gave a sovereign to his wife.

He was not to return alive.

Calling at the *Cutthorpe Hotel*, which at one time he had owned, he met his neighbour and fellow-butcher Charles Hancock, and the pair had a drink for which Herbert paid. He wanted Hancock to go with him to Killamarsh to look over the shop there, but Hancock had business of his own to conclude, and had to decline the offer. Herbert told him he had meant to go on to Clowne from Killamarsh, but now Hancock was unable to come with him he would go to Sheffield instead, and return to Killamarsh on his way back. Leaving the hotel, Herbert Crookes walked to Sheepbridge and caught the 11.50 am train to Sheffield, travelling in company with Elias Taylor, landlord of the *Queen's Hotel* at Newbold Moor, and the Whittington Moor butcher Isaac Hewitt. On reaching Sheffield, the three drank together at a public house, Crookes taking gin while the other two stuck to beer. Crookes was still in the public house when Taylor and Hewitt left.

Later on he encountered another butcher friend, Peter Champion, and they ate a meal together, going on to drink brandy and beer at the *Victoria Hotel*. Crookes asked about the times of trains for Killamarsh, and decided to take the one that left at 3.15. He was also interested in the result of a bet he had placed on the Lincolnshire Handicap which was being run that day. Champion accompanied him to the station, where Crookes caught a train. He was next seen at 5.45 pm on the return train journey by Edward Froggatt, who got off with him at Eckington. They drank at the *Sitwell Arms* at Renishaw, and Crookes walked on to Barlborough where he made a further stop at the *Royal Oak*. By now he had discovered that Lonely, the horse he had backed, had lost. Perhaps it was an omen of what was to come.

Herbert Crookes arrived in Clowne and visited two public houses, though this time he limited himself to drinking a 'split lemon' only. At 8.30 pm he called on the butcher William Woodhead, with whom he had a shared arrangement for buying and slaughtering cattle, and in the course of their conversation told him that he would be coming over with his family to live in Clowne the following day. Woodhead remarked that he would not like to walk home alone so late, but Crookes replied that he was not afraid. He had a glass of beer at the *Crown*, and went on to the *Angel Inn*, where he drank two gins. It was now around 9 pm, and Crookes declared that he would walk home by Staveley, following the path beside the Chesterfield Canal. Charles Layhe, a farm

Bluebank Wood, Brimington, probable scene of Herbert Crookes' murder 'by person or persons unknown.' Dennis Middleton

Wheeldon Mill Lock, Brimington, where the body of Herbert Crookes was found.
Dennis Middleton

labourer living at the inn, offered him a bed for the night, but Crookes refused, saying that his wife would be waiting for him. He left the inn at 9.10 pm, and made for home. After this, no-one saw Herbert Crookes alive. Evidently he was hoping to use the canal path as a shortcut home, skirting rather than passing directly through Brimington and Whittington to reach the farm at Cutthorpe. Around 11.30 pm, a guard on a Midland Railway train running close by the canal at Wheeldon Mill lock, Brimington, heard terrible screams from somewhere in the darkness beyond. The same screams were also heard by a young boy at the *New Inn*, which was situated only a matter of yards from the lock.

Next morning, at 5.40, three young men on their way to work along the canal towpath saw a hard, flat-crowned hat lying on the ground. Picking it up, they discovered it had a hole in the crown, and guessed that some drunken men must have been fighting there the night before. Scouring the area in the hope of finding spilled coins, they noticed signs of a struggle. Tussocks of grass had been torn up, as if someone had clutched at them, and the ground bore the imprint of a man having knelt down there. They also found fragments of glass from a broken bottle. Following footprints towards the canal, they caught sight of a body floating in the backwater. With the help of two other men, Charles Brown and Henry Johnson, the three youths fixed a rope to the corpse and hauled it from the water. By the time the local constable P C Arthur Wright arrived, he was able to identify the dead man as Herbert Crookes. The body showed obvious signs of a violent attack and robbery, with the buttons and collar torn from the shirt and the pockets turned inside out. No money was recovered from the water.

At the subsequent inquest, as the witnesses gave their testimony, it became clear what had happened. Herbert Crookes must have been waylaid near the Blue Bank plantation on the other side of the canal path, with more than one man taking part in the assault. He had put up a fight, and bruising around the ribs showed he had taken a number of hard blows from his assailants. A mark on his forehead that may have come from being struck by a stick, or possibly the broken bottle, indicated that he might have been rendered unconscious. It is to be hoped so, for the robbers then dragged him from the plantation, and after rifling his pockets, callously pitched his body into the canal. Herbert Crookes had died, not from the vicious beating he was given, but from drowning in the water.

In spite of the claims of some witnesses who presented a saintly picture of a sober, restrained person not given to betting, the events of the day are enough to show that Herbert Crookes was not averse to a flutter on the horses, liked his drink – a fact confirmed by the state of his liver at the postmortem – and was generous with his money. It was thought that on the 24 March he set off with anything from £40 to £70 on his person, and the chances are that he made the fact rather too obvious to someone prior to returning home. Apparently he had almost been robbed on an earlier occasion, when his collie dog had given warning of three would-be thieves waiting in ambush on the road near Troughbrook Hill outside Staveley, and he had wisely taken a

The Mill Inn, *Brimington, formerly the* Prince of Wales, *where the inquest on Herbert Crookes was held.* Dennis Middleton

different way home. Unfortunately, this time the dog had not been there to help him.

Betrayed by his own overconfidence, and the greed of desperate men, Herbert Crookes had no hope. Alone and helpless in the dark, he perished in the murky waters of the Chesterfield Canal. The inquest jury needed no more than twenty minutes to return their verdict of wilful murder against 'some person or persons unknown.'

The verdict still stands. In spite of a thorough police investigation, the killers were never found. The death of Herbert Crookes remains unavenged.

CHAPTER 4

Murder in Barracks Yard
1888

Arthur Thomas Delaney was not a man to make friends easily. From the time of his apprenticeship with Messrs Oliver and Company to his current employment as a fitter with Plowright Brothers' engineering foundry at Brampton, he was known to his workmates as a moody, hard-drinking loner prone to outbursts of violence and best left to himself. For the last few months Delaney had been living at No 2 Barracks Yard with his wife and their infant child, but the marriage had been troubled from the outset. Some months ago Mrs Delaney had been granted a separation order by the Chesterfield magistrates, following a vicious assault by her husband, and had only returned to him after he promised to mend his ways. The reform, if genuine, had been short-lived, and early in April 1888 Delaney had made a further violent attack on his wife, which would appear to have included an indecent sexual assault of some kind. Hauled before the magistrates, he escaped with a fine, but evidently the punishment left him with a simmering resentment, and the desire to be revenged on his long-suffering wife. Delaney would later claim that he had decided to murder her as soon

Vicar Lane, Chesterfield, the view east from Low Pavement. Here, in Barrack Yard, Arthur Delaney battered his wife to death in 1888. Dennis Middleton

as he left the dock, and it was only a matter of days before he put his dreadful threats into practice.

Barracks Yard was one of several in the maze of courts and alleyways leading off Vicar Lane on its way from the Market Place to the junction with St Mary's Gate. Part of the grim, rundown centre of the Victorian town, it had formerly housed the Derbyshire Militia, who had given the place its name. The Delaney household had come to be known as 'Dark Hole', and it was to prove a not unfitting title for the place where savage murder would be done.

On 21 April 1888, Arthur Delaney and his wife crossed Vicar Lane to drink together at the *Red Lion Inn*. Delaney had been drinking heavily for several days before, seemingly nerving himself in readiness for the terrible deed, and in the course of their time at the *Red Lion* he told his wife that he would murder her before the night was out. Mrs Delaney treated this outburst as a joke, laughing and replying that he dare not do any such thing. She should have known her husband better.

She went home soon afterwards, but he stayed on, not returning until midnight. Delaney then gave his wife a shilling and asked her to go and get something for his supper. Drunk as he was, he must have known the shops would be closed, but perhaps this was part of his strategy. Mrs Delaney set off to look, only to find the shops had long since shut, and came back to tell her husband.

At this point Delaney made her hand him the door key, and locked the door. Then he launched a savage attack on her, grabbing the kitchen poker and raining blows on her head. The poor woman, still holding the baby in one hand, raised the other to ward off the onslaught, but it did her no good. Delaney struck her with such vicious force that the end was knocked clean off her ring finger, which was itself broken, and the middle finger badly injured. Her terrified screams brought the neighbours running, and were heard across the road by Fred Keeton, landlord of the *Red Lion*. He hurried into Barracks Yard, where a man called McHugh told him 'Delaney is butchering his wife.'

Unable to open the locked door, Keeton broke his way in to be met by a nauseating sight. Mrs Delaney lay on the floor unconscious in a pool of blood, still holding the year-old baby in her arm. The child was unhurt, but the face of the woman was a hideous mask of blood, her nose, forehead and left eye battered in from repeated blows. Arthur Delaney stood with his back to the fire, looking on apparently unmoved, and near him was the bloodstained poker. In the absence of a policeman, Keeton showed himself to be determined and resolute. He seized the poker, collared Delaney and marched him over to the police station in a citizen's arrest. Meanwhile Dr George Booth (the then Mayor of Chesterfield) and Dr Shea attended the luckless wife, and had her removed to Chesterfield Hospital. Though the staff there did their best, it was clear she would not survive. The frontal bone of the forehead had been driven in, exposing the brain, her left eye destroyed, her nasal and finger bones broken, and a great deal of blood lost. Amazingly, she lingered on for several weeks, finally dying on 12 July.

From the time he was arrested, Delaney made no attempt to deny that he was the killer. Although at first, when questioned as to why he had done the terrible deed, he answered that 'now was not the place to say', he later gave full details of the murderous plan he had hatched on Tuesday 17 April and had steeled himself to carry out four days later. At one stage he accused his wife of having been unfaithful with other men, but in the end he withdrew the accusation. Given the facts, the verdict of wilful murder by the coroner's jury was a foregone conclusion.

Brought to trial at the Derby Summer Assizes before Mr Justice Hawkins, Delaney must have known his fate. His brutal attack was not unlike that of William Goddard on his defenceless wife six years before, but while Goddard could claim not to have intended murder, Delaney had already confessed to having planned the killing. For him, there could be no escape, and he was sentenced to death.

In his last days Delaney was calm and restrained, expressing remorse for his brutal actions and anxious to clear his dead wife of any blame. The night before his execution he stood at the window of his cell, gazing out at the sky until it grew dark. He met his end on the gallows at Derby Gaol on Friday 10

Map of Vicar Lane, showing Militia Barracks, Red Lion Inn *and* Commercial Hotel. Ordnance Survey Sheet XXV.6.9, edition of 1878, Scale 1:500. Reproduced from the 1878 Ordnance Survey map. Chesterfield Local Studies Library

August 1888, wearing the same suit in which he had been arrested. Throughout the trial he had been resigned to his fate. Just before the executioner slipped the white cap over his head, Arthur Delaney was heard to utter his last words: 'Lord Jesus, have mercy on my soul.'

CHAPTER 5

A Most Terrible Charge
1888

I n November 1887, Mary Ann Whitfield came to live at Whitebank Yard (also known as Mill Yard) in Hasland with her engine driver husband and their four children. Their new neighbours couldn't help noticing that Mrs Whitfield was 'an untidy woman, and much given to drink', and seemed rarely to be sober, but she always treated her children kindly, and they appeared to be fit and healthy. The first disturbing signs appeared in June 1888, when the

Map of Birdholme area, then in Hasland parish, showing Whitebank Cottages on Derby Road, where in 1888 two young boys were poisoned by their mother, Mary Whitfield. Ordnance Survey Sheet XXV.10, edition of 1898, Scale 1:2500. Reproduced from the Ordnance Survey map. Chesterfield Local Studies Library

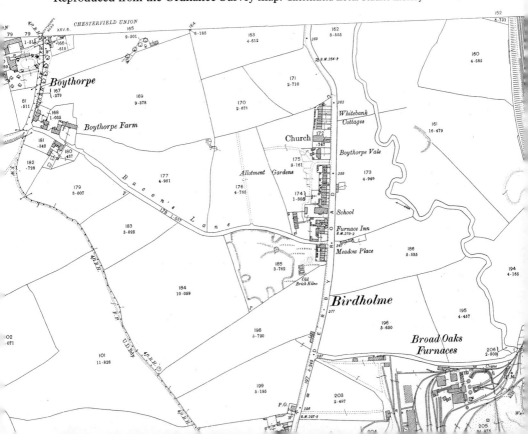

ten-year-old Alfred Vickers Whitfield was taken ill. His mother made a point of looking after him personally, preparing his food herself, but this seemed to do Alfred no good. When Dr Shea was called later that month the child was run down and lethargic, constipated and prone to vomiting, with a strangely puffy, swollen face. The medical man found albumen in the child's urine, which he thought must indicate a kidney disease, and prescribed medicine for it, but soon afterwards Alfred was racked with convulsions, and on 10 June he died. Death was diagnosed as being due to nephritis, and Dr Shea provided a death certificate. Barely two weeks later, his younger brother, eight-year-old Ernest Whitfield, also became unwell. Seen happily playing on 25 June, the following day he suddenly cried out in pain, fell to the ground and began to retch. He was laid on the sofa, where he scratched at his head, and asked his mother to put some laudanum on it. Elizabeth Rawson, a neighbour, was present in the house, and saw Mrs Whitfield return with a glass of yellowish liquid which she claimed was brandy and water, but Ernest, apparently recognising what it was, refused it, and his mother offered to drink it herself. Mrs Rawson did not see her drink from the glass. After suffering convulsions, and an unpleasant brown discharge from his nose and mouth, Ernest lapsed into unconsciousness and died on

Church of St Augustine, Derby Road. Ann Krawszik

Derby Road at its junction with St Augustine's Road. Houses occupying the former Whitebank Cottages site are shown on far right. Ann Krawszik

27 June. Maud Rawson, Elizabeth's daughter, reported having seen the same symptoms in Alfred, as she was in the house before he died.

Coming so soon after the death of his elder brother, Ernest's demise aroused suspicion. Both Dr Shea and his partner Dr Jeffreys attended the younger child before his death, and the latter advised that no certificate be provided. In his view, the symptoms were consistent with narcotic poisoning. Dr Shea, in spite of evident misgivings, awarded the certificate, which gave the cause of death as congestion of the lungs. It was probably Dr Jeffreys who, on leaving, was overheard by the neighbours to remark that 'twelve men will sit' before a certificate was provided, indicating that an inquiry into the death would be required. When this news was passed on to Mrs Whitfield she became angry and defiant, swearing a great deal and declaring that she did not care 'if twenty men should sit.' Later, just before Ernest's funeral in Hasland Cemetery, she was seen to be 'rather intoxicated'.

On 4 February 1889 Harry Whitfield found his mother lying unconscious in the attic, and a laudanum bottle from which she had drunk in what was clearly an attempt at suicide. Beside her were two farewell notes, addressed to Mr Whitfield and to the surviving children. By now she was clearly a murder suspect, and was taken into custody. At the inquest, held at the Municipal Hall in Chesterfield, a number of disturbing facts emerged. The jury learned that the Whitfields had insured the lives of the two dead boys with the Wesleyan and General Insurance Society, and that young Alfred had signed and completed the insurance form himself. Having a child sign a form which he was obviously incapable of understanding fully was suspicious enough in itself, and it is unlikely that the jury were any less uneasy when Charles Dolman, the Clay Cross agent for the Society, reported that he or members of his family had paid out the insurance money to Mrs Whitfield on being presented with the death certificates. Mr Whitfield had signed to acknowledge receipt, and afterwards agreed to write a testimonial for the Society. Mrs Rawson, who had been present when the money was paid, confirmed the Dolmans' testimony.

Even more sinister were the unexplained bouts of illness suffered by Mr Whitfield after the death of Ernest. During the Christmas of 1888, Mrs Whitfield had tried to borrow money, claiming that her husband's clothes were in pawn and needed to be redeemed. Refused the money, she replied that 'he would have to be a prisoner' today, and in fact Mr Whitfield had been

South Place, Chesterfield, adjoining Bowling Green and former site of Municipal Hall, where an inquest was held on the poisoned Whitfield boys. Ann Krawszik

ill for the day, apparently losing the use of his legs and being unable to see for a short time. Similar attacks had been suffered at other times, and Harry Whitfield confirmed that these had always taken place when his father had a day off work. On each occasion, the symptoms were remarkably similar to those seen in the two children. Since his wife had been arrested, Mr Whitfield had been free of these unusual health problems.

Before the inquest took place, the bodies of both Alfred and Ernest were exhumed from the Hasland Cemetery, and their internal organs examined by Dr William Fielden, of Chesterfield, and by the county analyst Alfred Henry Allen. No suspicious traces were found in Alfred's remains, but those of Ernest revealed a small quantity of meconic acid, a body peculiar to opium. Since opium, which could be administered as laudanum, was a poison absorbed fairly quickly by the body, the presumption had to be that a much larger quantity of opium had been ingested prior to death. It also meant that it was possible that Alfred could have been poisoned in the same way, but as he had been longer in the ground the poison had been totally absorbed and disappeared. The coroner's jury brought a verdict of wilful murder.

Mary Ann Whitfield came to trial at the 1889 Derbyshire Summer Assizes, charged with the murder of her son Ernest Whitfield, and with the further criminal offence of attempting suicide. Once more the witnesses, including the medical experts, gave their evidence, and Mr Etherington Smith presented the case for the prosecution. Defence counsel Mr Hextall replied with an emotional speech, imploring the jurors to see how unbelievable it was that a mother could be guilty of this 'most terrible charge', and poison her own children for such relatively small sums of money. His argument was noticeably short on facts and long on feeling, but he may well have scored when, in concluding his speech, he reminded the jury that their decision would affect the lives of the husband and two surviving children as much as that of their mother. Whatever the reason, the jury came back against all the odds with a verdict of 'not guilty', and Mary Ann Whitfield was acquitted! For the attempted suicide, there was less forgiveness, and the judge sentenced her to four months hard labour.

St Paul's Church, Hasland. Ann Krawszik

The decision caused shock and outrage in Chesterfield, where at first it was thought there must have been some mistake in the reporting of the case. Nevertheless, it was true. There is surely little doubt that she murdered her two sons, and attempted to kill her husband, for the paltry reward of a few pounds of insurance money, no doubt in order to buy drink. What went through the minds of the Assizes jury we cannot know, but it seems likely that – in common with other jury members of trials already reported – they disliked condemning a fellow human being to death, and that they did not wish to let a woman hang for murder. Whatever the reason for their verdict, Mary Ann Whitfield was free to return to her family after four months in prison. One cannot help feeling, though, that in future the Whitfields would have kept a close eye on the laudanum bottle, and it is doubtful that any of them would have had a taste for brandy and water.

Hasland Cemetery, last resting place of poison victims Alfred and Ernest Whitfield. Ann Krawszik

CHAPTER 6

So Sad and Terrible a Deed
1889

F or close on eight months, George Horton had been a widower. His wife had died in October 1888, leaving him to care for their seven children on his own. Given his arduous work as a miner at the new Alfreton pit, and his liking for drink, it is not surprising that by May 1889 the burden of being a lone parent had begun to weigh upon him. Presently, he would seek the deadliest of solutions to his problem.

By 1889 Horton had managed to farm out two of his large family, his fifteen-year-old daughter and a four-year-old living away from home. He and the other five lived at the village of Swanwick, a mining settlement south-east of Alfreton. Their home was a building made from two converted cottages, which the Hortons shared with Henry and Ann Bowskill and their children, both families making use of the downstairs area but keeping to separate upstairs rooms. Horton and his children had the use of two bedrooms, he himself sharing a room with his son Joseph and eight-year-old daughter Kate, while the second room was occupied by Sarah Jane (thirteen), George (ten) and Charlotte (five).

On the evening of 19 May, Kate and Joseph went to bed at 7.15, and their father followed about 10.30, passing through the room that housed the other children to get there. Early next morning, before 6 o'clock, Mr Bowskill knocked on the wall to wake up Horton for his shift at the colliery. Soon afterwards Sarah Jane heard her father get out of bed, and the voice of her sister Kate asking him for a drink. Horton replied that she must go downstairs and get one for herself, as he would be late for work if he stayed. Then he walked through the second bedroom, and went down the stairs.

Perhaps half an hour later Kate came into the room and lay on Sarah Jane's bed, and complained of pains in her belly and bowels. Her hands were clenched tight, and her legs and arms became stiff. Kate began to shake with convulsive spasms, and her terrified sister ran to fetch Mrs Bowskill from next door. Seeing the serious condition of the child, the latter sent for Dr Bingham from Alfreton, but Kate Horton was beyond help by the time he arrived. She died quickly, and in great pain, at 7 am, her last moments witnessed by Mrs Bowskill and another neighbour, Ann Evans. Before dying, she told them that 'dadda had given her some blue stuff out of a cup.' Mrs Bowskill made a search of the bedroom, but was unable to find evidence of any kind of poisonous substance.

Horton, who had set off to work, returned unexpectedly at 8.30 am, to be told by little Charlotte that Kate was dead. He seemed very distressed, weeping over the body and kissing the dead face. When Mrs Evans repeated Kate's dying words to him he vehemently denied doing any such thing. Testifying later at the Assizes, Mrs Evans would recall that, although Kate was suffering considerable pain, she was definitely fully conscious when she had made the statement.

Foul play was suspected, and Dr Bingham acted almost immediately. When Horton came to him at 9.30 that same morning and asked for a death certificate, the doctor refused to provide it. Bingham carried out a postmortem on the dead girl the following day, and found a collection of blue particles in Kate's stomach and intestines. The organs, and traces of dark brown matter from the child's mouth, were passed to P C O'Connor, who handed them on for the expert attention of Mr A H Allen, the analyst. Subjecting the remains to chemical analysis, Mr Allen found what Bingham had suspected, that Kate had died from strychnine poisoning. From the amount found, and allowing for absorption by the body, Allen estimated that two grains had been ingested, more than enough to cause death. The blue particles in the stomach and intestines he identified as ultramarine, a colouring agent used with strychnine in the preparation of vermin-killing powders available in local shops. In view of the rapid effect of the poison, it was his opinion that Kate had taken the poison an hour or so before her death.

Her father was the obvious suspect. George Horton was arrested on 28 May and charged with the murder of his daughter. He replied that he had nothing to say. By the time he was brought to the Derbyshire Summer Assizes, a number of other witnesses were ready to provide further damning – albeit circumstantial – evidence. His eldest daughter, Annie Elizabeth Horton, had left home two months before Kate died. Two months before that, she claimed that her father had warned her that 'he would poison her out of the road'. According to Annie, it was this fear of being poisoned that had made her leave the house. David Shaw, a fellow collier, testified that some weeks before the death, he had overheard Horton say that he had already 'got shut' of two children, and would 'get shut' of the rest, and would then 'take his hook'. Young George also gave evidence, stating how his father had hit him as punishment for telling his schoolfriends that Horton had given the 'blue stuff' for Kate to drink before she died. Horton had also been seen on the morning of the murder coming out from a plantation that was out of his way, a strange place to be visited by a man already late for work. Evidence was heard from the Bowskills, Mrs Evans, Dr Bingham and Mr Allen, and Sarah Jane Horton.

A possible motive had also emerged. Kate Horton had been insured with the Refuge Insurance Company, and her father could expect to collect £7 for her death. Apparently there had initially been some reluctance on the part of the public prosecutor to proceed with the murder charge, and it is easy to see why. In spite of the mass of circumstantial testimony, and the fact that Kate Horton was undoubtedly a victim of strychnine poisoning, no trace was found of poison in the house, and there was nothing to positively connect her father with what was described in court as 'so sad and terrible a deed.' Nevertheless, the evidence provided convinced the jury, who returned a guilty verdict. In answer, Horton continued to assert his innocence. The judge then donned the black cap, and passed the sentence of death upon him. Ironically, Horton appeared before the same jury that acquitted Mary Ann Whitfield on what was virtually an identical charge.

On Wednesday 7 August Horton was visited in his cell by Reverend J E Matthews, and confessed to the murder of his child. He told the clergyman that he had bought some rat poison which he then dissolved in a bottle, hiding it in readiness until 20 May, when he had given it to the thirsty Kate as a lethal drink in a cup. His visit to the plantation had been to hide the bottle there, away from the house. Mounting debts, made worse by his earlier drinking habits, had made the £7 insurance money a fatal attraction, and for this paltry sum his young daughter had paid with her life.

Two weeks later, on the morning of Wednesday 21 August, George Horton made his last walk to the scaffold at Derby Gaol. He appeared to have aged a great deal since the time of his trial, and had lost weight, but it was reported that he had slept well and had eaten a hearty breakfast that morning. He declined the routine offer of a chair, and walked calmly to the middle of the drop. Just before he died, he was heard to say: 'Oh Lord, receive my soul.' Then the drop fell, and the Swanwick poisoner had paid for his daughter's suffering.

Swanwick village, where in 1889 miner George Horton murdered his daughter Kate with a cup of cyanide. Dennis Middleton

CHAPTER 7

God Bless Thee; Good Morning 1890

Edward French and his wife Mary Ann were the partners in a troubled marriage. That much had been plain to most of their neighbours in Eckington from the time the couple had moved to the village four months ago. They had been married for nine years, and had seven children, the youngest a pair of infant twins, but this did not seem to promote any other kind of harmony between husband and wife. French, who was fond of drink and gambling, got into the habit of inviting his friends to the house to imbibe and play cards until the early hours, and before very long the gossip was going round the village that Mary Ann was entertaining admirers other than her husband.

As with most rumours of this kind, any hard evidence was notable for its absence, but it was enough to enrage Edward French once he started to hear of it. His jealous nature was well known, and it was not long before he reacted violently, beating and abusing his wife. Unable to bear this treatment any longer, Mary Ann left their house and returned to Barlborough to live with her mother in Talbot Yard. Intriguingly enough, her mother's name was also Mary

West Street, Eckington, for a time the home of Edward and Mary French. Dennis Middleton

French, as she had married her son-in-law's brother John French following the death of her first husband. Edward French also left the home, going to an unspecified Yorkshire village to make a fresh start. According to the testimony of his mother-in-law later on, he earned good money there, but managed to spend most of it on gambling and drink.

Some months later, in July 1890, Edward French reappeared in Eckington, living in West Street at the house of his collier friend William Gee, who was also married to his sister Sarah. During the next few weeks he had several chance meetings with Mary Ann, and although he warned her that he would 'do for her' on one occasion, his wife seemed to think that this was a mere empty threat.

On the morning of Saturday 2 August 1890 Edward French called on his wife and mother-in-law at their home in Talbot Yard, Barlborough. At first he was met with suspicion, not surprising in view of his previous visits, when he had usually been abusive and threatening, but this time French promised the two women he was tired of his present mode of life, and intended to turn over a new leaf. He was going to look for work in Barlborough, he told them, and cupping Mary Ann's chin he informed her fondly: 'My lass, we are going to lead a different life now.' Their earlier problems he blamed on two women, presumably the main purveyors of gossip in the village.

Mary Ann responded that if she did return to him, 'I shall not have a dog's life again. I can't be knocked about as I have been.' French urged her to forgive and forget, and, quickly changing the subject, told her he would need a shave before he went to seek out work. He asked the elder Mary French if 'our Jack' had a razor, and his mother-in-law fetched it and handed it to him. She also gave him hot water to shave. When French went out, he was shaved, but she did not see the razor again until it was produced in court. By then it had been put to a terrible use.

French came home again about 11 am, and informed the women that he had secured a job at Staveley colliery, and was to start work on Monday. When his brother John invited him out for a drink, Edward declined, replying that he meant to

The village of Barlborough, where, in Talbot Yard, Mary French met a terrible death. Dennis Middleton

lead a different kind of life. He stayed in the house all that day and ate his meals, not taking anything stronger than a glass of porter at supper. Earlier on, he had sent a boy out to collect his pit clothes and tools for work at Staveley colliery. He didn't eat much either, and when his worried wife urged him to do so, French told her: 'I have not been able to eat much since we parted, all through my foolish tongue.' John French, who had come in after imbibing freely, went to bed before midnight, and Edward asked his mother-in-law why she did not go up to join him. He told her he was not going to bed. Mrs French obligingly brought him down some pillows, and he bedded down on the sofa. When his mother-in-law eventually went upstairs, he was still lying there while his wife raked out the fire. Husband and wife were talking together, and they were not arguing for once. No doubt the older woman thought that things might be getting better, after all.

About 1.30 am Mrs French heard her daughter call out 'Mother!' twice; it was not a scream, but all the same she knew it meant trouble. Hurrying downstairs, she found Mary Ann lying behind the stairs, and blood running through into the passage. Peering through the half-open door, Mrs French cried out 'Oh, Ted! You've murdered my child!' and Edward French came to the door and barred her way, telling her he would do the same to her if she raised the alarm before he got clear. He went back into the room, and into the street, and his mother-in-law heard him say that she would find him 'in Foxton dam, the canal, or on the line.' Once he was gone, Mrs French managed to get out of the house. The frightened woman ran through the village crying: 'Murder!' Returning, she caught sight of French disappearing round a corner to his brother William's house.

Mrs French went back to her own house, followed by the neighbours and the local constable, P C Ryan. They found Mary Ann French lying dead on her back, near to the sofa, in a spreading pool of blood. Her throat had been cut, and the blood-splashed room itself resembled a slaughterhouse. William James Anderson, the surgeon from Clowne, arrived at 2 am. Examining the dead woman, he found that a gaping wound had been inflicted, extending almost from ear to ear, and cutting through almost to the spine. Such was the amount of force used, the jugular veins and the upper part of the windpipe had been cut, and the head almost severed from the body. Anderson also found another superficial wound to the neck, and cuts on the fingers, showing that Mary Ann had tried vainly to ward off the blows. The wounds were consistent with the bloodstained razor, which was recovered from under a bucket outside the house. Anderson concluded that death must have been instantaneous, and that 'it would take a pretty strong arm to make the wound.' Jealousy had, it seemed, lent an added strength to French as he struck the lethal blow.

Edward French arrived at the home of his brother William about 1.45 that Sunday morning. By the standards of the time he was in a state of undress, wearing only trousers and shirt, and with no boots on his feet. More disturbing still, his hands and arms were splashed to the elbows with blood, and one hand was badly cut. Edward informed his horrified brother that he had 'done it', and that he was going on to see his mother and sisters. William tried to pull him inside the house, but Edward broke away, telling him: 'Nay, I won't. God bless thee; good morning.' Then he was gone. William was not to see him alive again. French went on to Eckington, making further calls at the homes of collier Samuel Mallinder and Edward's in-laws,

Plumbley, near Barlborough, where Edward French took his own life after murdering his wife. Dennis Middleton

the Gees. At the latter place he spoke to his sister Sarah and to his mother, telling them he had killed his wife. Like William French, they were shocked. Unlike John French, who felt that Edward had used the supposed infidelity of his wife to excuse his own jealousy, William and the Gees seemed to think that Mary Ann probably had been unfaithful to her husband, but all of them had urged him to return to her as 'the best thing he could do' and were now appalled at the awful turn of events.

Kissing his mother, Edward bade her farewell, informing her she would never see him again. He then made for Foxton Dam, intending to drown himself, but seeing someone on the road decided him against it. French crossed the turnpike on to a bridle path that led through three fields, crossing the Plumbley colliery branch line towards the Boiley Bridge that overhung the Midland line between Eckington and Killamarsh. He climbed the fence and the railway embankment, going to the far side of the line near the bridge. He must then have waited for the first train to appear, and lain carefully down with his head and neck resting on the line.

At 4.25 am, James Innes was the guard on a Midland train running from Killamarsh to Eckington. The driver was hailed by the guard of another train, who reported that there was something on the line. Pulling up, Innes and the driver found the lifeless body of Edward French lying short of the metals, while the severed head lay in the 'four-foot' beyond. Evidently he had deliberately placed himself in the path of a passing train in order to end his life.

When the double inquest opened on Tuesday 5 August, a large crowd surrounded the *Royal Oak Inn* at Barlborough where the unfortunate Mary Ann French had been laid out. Although made more presentable, the sight of her corpse roused great emotion in witnesses and jury alike, and several broke down in tears while giving and hearing testimony. Later that day the remains of Edward French were examined by the jury at the *Sitwell Arms* in Renishaw, where once again hundreds of onlookers fought for a glimpse of the 'not very enviable sight'. His brother William French viewed him here for the last time. Overcome with grief, William picked up the severed head, severely battered by the couplings of passing trucks, and kissed the dead lips in a grisly and moving farewell. Edward French had by his own confession committed murder, and ended his life by suicide. The possibility of insanity was also raised. Both John and William French felt that their brother had behaved strangely in the recent past, and at one time the latter had become worried that Edward would be 'going to Mickleover' (the local mental hospital). The Coroner's view was that there was no evidence whatsoever that French had been insane, as he had acted in a premeditated and deliberate fashion, and done exactly what he said he would do. In the end, and after some disagreement, the jury returned a verdict of *felo de se*.

Sadly, for Edward and Mary Ann French, their decision no longer mattered.

Royal Oak Inn, *Barlborough, where the inquest jury and witnesses wept as the body of Mary Ann French was laid out for inspection.* Dennis Middleton

Chapter 8

A Gunshot at the Window
1891

Michael Thomas Morrall and his wife Martha were well known to most people in Matlock. The elderly couple, both in their seventies, had for many years lived in relative isolation at their home, Balmoral House, on Bent Lane in the area known as Matlock Bank, on the hill above Matlock itself. Mr Morrall had moved here thirty years ago, following his retirement from the Redditch needle-manufacturing firm of Abel Morrall and Company on payment of an annuity of £150 a year, and had since enlarged his new home. The house, an eerily striking two-storey structure with diamond-shaped window lights, stood stark and alone among the surrounding fields and woods, 600 feet above sea level overlooking the town, and the Morralls received only occasional visitors.

Both husband and wife were staunch Quakers, and Mr Morrall was regarded as something of an eccentric. His tall, soberly-garbed figure was a familiar sight at Jesse Davis's Poplar Cottage Hydropathic Establishment, where he was a frequent visitor, demonstrating his skill at the 'rubbing cure'. He was also a regular attender at the Friends Meeting House, where he had made a number of impressive speeches. Witty, talkative and amusing, he was usually welcomed by those locals he decided to engage in conversation. True, it was said that in the past he had suffered from mental problems, and just after Christmas 1890 he had spent some time in Smedley's Memorial Hospital to be treated for a 'nervous derangement', but he had since returned to his home with no obvious ill effects. To be sure, he was eccentric, but harmless enough. Michael Morrall and his wife were the last couple anyone in Matlock would have associated with an act of murder.

On the night of Thursday 26 March 1891, between 9 and 10 pm, Mr Morrall bade his wife goodnight and retired to bed. Martha Morrall remained in the kitchen, seated in a low rocking-chair in front of the fire. She was reading the newspaper.

Soon afterwards, Martha Smith, a nurse at the Rockside Hydropathic Establishment on Cavendish Road, a hundred yards or so from Balmoral House, was on her way downstairs to tend to a patient when she heard the sound of a gunshot. The noise was quite clear and distinct, and her immediate thought was that someone must be poaching in the fields above Cavendish Road. No-one else at Rockside heard the shot, as a party was being staged for patients, staff and guests, and music and dancing was taking place in the grounds. Nurse Smith, though, was not the only one to hear it. George Wall, a stone cutter, was standing in the road near to Rockside when he also heard the gunshot, coming from the direction of Balmoral House. Like her, Wall did not regard it as anything suspicious, putting it down to some late-night 'sportsman'.

At about the same time Henry Smith was returning home with his young daughter along Cavendish Road. Approaching the badly lit area of Bent Lane and its adjoining fields, the child remarked on a bright light showing at Balmoral House. Mr Smith assumed that the old couple, who had dispensed

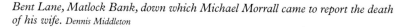

Bent Lane, Matlock Bank, down which Michael Morrall came to report the death of his wife. Dennis Middleton

with the services of a servant some months ago, must have forgotten to lower the window blind.

The first hint that something was wrong came at around 10.30 pm, when Mr Morrall rang the porter's bell at Rockside. Entering, he was coming down the corridor when he was met by Joseph Rowlett, the 'boots'. The old gentleman appeared quite agitated, and told Rowlett that there had been 'an explosion' at Balmoral House, his wife was dead, and he wanted someone to return with him to the house. Mr Morrall did not wait, but turned immediately for home. It was already beginning to snow as Rowlett, with two stablemen Henry Bradshaw and James Green, hurried up to the house on Bent Lane, but not seeing Mr Morrall anywhere, they were reluctant to go inside. The three went back to the entrance gates and waited until Mr Morrall arrived. He had been to the Poplar Cottage hydro, and informed the proprietor Mr Davis of what had happened.

The three men were directed to the front door by Mr Morrall, who opened it from inside to let them in. Going through the unlit parlour to the kitchen, where a single candle was burning, they found Martha Morrall lolling dead in her chair by the fire. She had a wound in the right side of the head, turned towards the window, and blood poured down the left side of her face to join a dark, spreading pool on the floor. Mr Morrall looked around the room, and told them he couldn't find out where the explosion had come from. He claimed he had been getting into bed, and had come downstairs on hearing 'a crackling noise', only to find the body of his wife. Rowlett noticed that the window blind was three or four inches from the top, and that a flower pot on the window sill had fallen over. He was told it had been blown down. He and the other two men were shown out by Mr Morrall, who was still standing in the doorway when they left. As they walked home it began to snow more heavily.

Having overheard a chance remark that a woman had been murdered, Sergeant Ramshall left the Matlock police station and arrived at Balmoral House just after 11 pm. Examining the body, he found that Mrs Morrall had a very large head wound, on the right side near the temple. Her tongue, which protruded from her mouth, had been badly cut, and a pool of clotted blood stained the floor and the fallen newspaper. A pair of spectacles lay in the blood, the right glass entirely smashed, and the lid of the spectacle case was on the table, near to an overturned flower pot. Like Joseph Rowlett, he noticed that the blind was drawn up to within a few inches of the top of the window. Ramshall also observed that it was singed at the bottom, and that two panes of window glass had been broken, leaving glass fragments on the floor. He found evidence of sulphur from gunsmoke, and the marks of scattered shot in the door and the table, indicating that a gun had been fired. Investigating further, he found broken window glass outside near a flower-bed four feet from the window, and marks on the sill where a firearm had been placed on it. From what he could make out, the blind had been drawn down, and must have flown up when hit – and burned – by the discharge, which would explain the scattering of shot. It would also have caused the bright light seen by Henry Smith and his daughter.

Going through to the parlour, Ramshall discovered that a glass pane in the book-case had been broken, and that a poker and a box of dominoes were lying on a table nearby. He questioned Mr Morrall, who gave the same explanation as before, and showed the sergeant his bed, which indicated that someone had been lying on it. Apparently surprised by the scene in the parlour, he claimed that someone must have broken in and smashed the glass to get the domino box from the book-case, mistakenly assuming it to be a cash-box. When Ramshall pointed out that there was no sign of forced entry anywhere, he replied that he or his wife had probably forgotten to lock the doors. Given that his wife had just been killed, he appeared remarkably unconcerned. In view of the suspicious circumstances, it was decided that Mr Morrall should be put in the care of an officer, while another stayed at the house. Meanwhile, further investigation was hampered by a heavy snowstorm, which obliterated any tracks that might have been left by the assassin. Whoever he was, he had evidently taken care to stand on paving slabs rather than grass, and would probably have left few prints behind him.

When the inquest, begun on Saturday, re-opened at Balmoral House on Monday 6 April, a crowd of newsmen besieged the entrance, fighting to get inside, and the venue was eventually moved to the billiard room at Rockside, in order to accommodate everyone. Medical evidence was provided by the Morrall family physician, Dr Moxon, whose post-mortem findings corroborated much of Sergeant Ramshall's testimony. In his opinion, death had resulted from haemorrhage from the huge head wound, caused by 'the discharge of small shot from a firearm', which had shattered the lower facial bones and caused extensive damage to the skull. Other shots had lodged in the fingers of the victim's left hand, and charring on her clothing suggested that she had fallen forward when hit, and been burned by the fire, although Moxon felt that it would have taken a good fire to ignite her woollen clothes.

From police examination of the murder scene, it appeared that the killer had crouched by the bottom pane of the window and taken a careful, deliberate aim, the shot breaking the pane and its concussion smashing the one above it. The shot had been fired at extremely close range, no more than four feet from the head of the victim. The murder weapon was evidently a gun, rather than a pistol, which must have been loaded with a heavy charge of small shot. Both triggers had been pulled together, and poor Mrs Morrall had taken the full impact. The firearm was never found, and apart from the shots inside the house, no other evidence was obtained. A cartridge discovered close to the house was produced, but proved to be an old one that bore no relation to the gun that killed Mrs Morrall.

Her husband, the obvious suspect, appeared at the inquest, where he was grilled at some length by the Coroner. He proved extremely vague in his replies, apparently unable to remember whether Rowlett and his companions had called on him or not, failing to recall what was said and done, and repeating his earlier claims that he had come downstairs on hearing the 'explosion' to find his wife dead and both doors wide open. His answers did not satisfy the Coroner, and the burglary theory obviously held no water. There was £100 in notes in the bedroom that remained untouched, no sign of forced entry, and no reason why a burglar should then go round to the front window and shoot Mrs Morrall through it.

On the other hand, there was nothing that directly linked Mr Morrall to the death of his wife. The couple's relationship had always seemed very cordial, and Mr Morrall a harmless eccentric who had never shown any tendency to violence. Samuel Brown of the Friends Society, who gave evidence earlier at the inquest, testified that Mr Morrall had been confined at the Friends' Retreat in York, and later at the County Asylum, some twelve years ago, but had never behaved violently, or been a danger to anyone but himself. He had never been seen to use a firearm, and no weapon was ever found at the house. Elderly and shaky in his limbs, he seemed a most unlikely fit for a killer who had crouched at the window and taken a calm, steady aim, the more so as the six-foot Mr Morrall would have had to stoop down to an unusual degree to reach the bottom pane. There was talk that the couple had received threatening letters in the past, one of which had led to a servant leaving the house, but this Mr Morrall denied. In the end, faced by a marked lack of evidence, and with a more than reasonable doubt, the inquest jury returned a verdict of wilful murder by a person or persons unknown.

Martha Morrall was seventy-seven when she died. The question as to who would want to murder an inoffensive old lady as she sat reading the paper in her rocking-chair remains unanswered. So, too, does the identity of her killer.

Rockside Hydropathic Establishment, Cavendish Road, Matlock, now a ruin, where witnesses first learned of the death of Mrs Martha Morrall. Dennis Middleton

CHAPTER 9

A Billhook in the Barn
1896

William Pugh was off work due to illness. At least, that was his story. He claimed he had 'a bad throat' and had not returned to his job at Shirland colliery since Easter. All the same, his illness did not prevent him from courting his fiancee Sarah Saunders, or for running the occasional errand on behalf of her mother. Pugh and Sarah were a long-standing 'item', but as yet he did not seem in any hurry to find a home for them, and was quite content to drop in from his lodgings for a regular spell of wooing. Pugh, a handsome young fellow of twenty-one, fancied himself as something of a ladies' man, and was hot-tempered and sensitive to insults. When he heard that Lizzie Boot had made adverse comments about his failure to do the right thing by Sarah, he reacted angrily, telling his informant that if he met her: 'I'll give her Lizzie Boot, that's all!'

Lizzie Boot had lived in with Thomas Limb as his housekeeper at Lindway Farm for just over three years. She

Holy Trinity Church, Brackenfield. Not far from here, at Lindway Farm, William Pugh murdered Lizzie Boot with a billhook in 1896. Dennis Middleton.

had gone to work for the thirty-six-year-old bachelor farmer from her own family farm in Brackenfield, having previously lived there with her widowed mother. Mr Limb was evidently more than satisfied with his young housekeeper, a pretty girl of nineteen, who proved a conscientious and hard-working employee. Although sought after by other young men from the village, Lizzie seemed to have no interest in the attentions of the opposite sex, let alone courtship and marriage. She was happy in her work, and sometimes her seven-year-old niece Beatrice Boot would come over to visit and keep her company. Lindway Farm, set off the beaten track along Lindway Lane some distance from Brackenfield village, was a secluded but picturesque spot, and to Lizzie it must have seemed an ideal situation. On Saturday 9 May 1896 Lizzie and her niece were alone in the house, Mr Limb having gone to the May Fair at Matlock. They had just finished eating their dinner when a knock came at the door. Beatrice went to answer it, and opened the door to find 'Billy Pugh' standing there. He asked to see her aunt, and the girl let him in. Pugh and her aunt had a brief conversation, but Beatrice did not hear what they said. Leaving her in the house, Lizzie and the young man went outside and walked down the farmyard to the barn. Lizzie Boot was not to come out of there alive.

Later on that afternoon George Hitchcock, a farm labourer, arrived from Ashover with a load of straw for weighing. Arriving outside the house, he caught sight of Pugh coming up the stackyard from the direction of the barn. On seeing Hitchcock the young man stopped and turned as if about to go back, then came on again. Hitchcock called out and asked if anyone else was about, and Pugh told him they were round the corner of the house. He then left the yard, while Hitchcock went round the side of the house. He saw Harry Towndrow walking up the field with the horses, but William Bryan, an elderly farm labourer, was at the bottom of the field. At Hitchcock's request, Bryan set off to the barn to find the 'troys' to weigh the straw with. Beatrice, who had come outside, followed the old farmhand into the barn.

Moments later Hitchcock saw the young girl come running out, obviously very distressed, crying out 'my auntie's dying!'

Behind her, old Bryan peered around the barn door and called to Hitchcock that here was 'a pretty sight', and to come and look. Hitchcock went to the barn and, looking in from outside, saw Lizzie Boot lying on her back in the barn, with blood near to her face. Deciding he had already seen enough, he shouted to Towndrow, who came running over. After Hitchcock had left, Towndrow saw Pugh coming up the stackyard with blood on his face and hands, and apparently in a very flustered state. He told Towndrow: 'the little girl says I've done it', and wiped at his face with a blue handkerchief. He then went into the field, and Towndrow did not see him again that day.

Hitchcock himself went off to get further assistance. On the way he met Mrs Saunders, a neighbour whose daughter Sarah was being courted by Pugh, and directed her to the barn before going on to enlist the aid of Miss Annie Greenhough further down the road. As he and Miss Greenhough were turning back for the farm, Hitchcock saw William Pugh walking along the path behind the Greenhough house as if on his way from where he lodged with Luke Wilson and his wife. On being told that something was wrong at the barn, Pugh appeared to know nothing about it, but accompanied Hitchcock and Miss Greenhough to Lindway Farm. Hitchcock then went to the Bennett household and instructed their son to go and fetch Thomas Limb. As it happened, the boy met the farmer already returning from Matlock a short time later.

Meanwhile, in the barn, William Bryan surveyed the ugly sight of the dead girl, who lay with her feet towards the barn door. The body showed a terrible, gaping wound in the throat that had all but severed her head, and a great trail of blood stained the floor of the barn around her. Bryan was still taking this in when Pugh came into the barn and stood looking at the corpse. Remarking that it was 'a bad job', he bent over the lifeless girl and appeared to gently stroke her cheek. As he did so, Bryan noticed a raw mark like a graze above the young man's left eye that seemed to be a fresh wound. Pugh suggested to Bryan that perhaps they ought to move the body, but the older man made no reply, and he did not attempt to do this himself. Inside the barn lay a billhook, smeared and

Brackenfield village, home of killer William Pugh in 1896. Ann Krawszik

splashed with blood. Pugh picked it up and, going outside, showed it to George Hitchcock, who had now returned to the farm, and telling him: 'this is what it was done with.' He was persuaded to take the billhook back and leave it where he found it, before going away again. Hitchcock, meanwhile, had noticed spots of blood on the ground at the point where Pugh had stopped and turned back when catching sight of him earlier that afternoon. A trail of similar spots led all the way back to the barn.

Word was sent to John and Harry Boot, brothers of the dead girl, and from what was told them they immediately suspected William Pugh. The two went to the Saunders house, where Pugh came calmly to the door, smoking, and denied all their accusations. John Boot noticed spots of blood on his wristbands, and asked him about it. Pugh claimed he had got them while helping Bryan move Lizzie's body. John Boot was far from satisfied, and he and his brother went to the barn and viewed his dead sister, finding out from other witnesses what they could. John then cycled to South Wingfield and informed the local constable, John Wilson. He and Boot returned to the Saunders house, where they found William Pugh at ease on the sofa beside his fiancee, Sarah Saunders. He was promptly arrested and taken into custody.

It later transpired that Pugh had been wearing a grey and orange striped shirt on his visit to Lindway Farm, but had gone back to his lodgings with the Wilsons and changed it. Luke Wilson and his wife found it upstairs, with what looked like bloodstains on the sleeves. Mrs Wilson was the sister of Sarah Saunders, and the couple were reluctant to believe their lodger was guilty. Not wanting to implicate him, they at first washed the shirt and then burned it, only coming forward later to testify. In spite of Pugh's efforts, there were blood spots on the wrists of his new shirt that were noticed by the Boots, and further stains were found on the sleeves and the back of his coat.

The inquest took place over Monday and Tuesday 11 and 12 May, and the numerous witnesses gave their evidence. Dr Walford of Stonebroom reported the results of his post-mortem. He told the jury that Lizzie Boot had died from haemorrhage caused by two distinct blows to the throat which had inflicted a five-inch gash, severed the air passage and the carotid artery, and penetrated almost to the bone. The wounds were consistent with the bloodstained billhook produced, and 'very great violence' had been used. The luckless girl had also suffered deep cuts on her hands, probably trying to protect herself from the billhook. The indications were that there had been a fierce struggle, with Lizzie trying to get to the door and the murderer barring her way. The doctor found no evidence of any sexual assault.

William Pugh continued to assert his innocence, and on Tuesday cross-questioned young Beatrice Boot, who appeared as a witness. The child, who nowadays would not have been put into so traumatic a situation, was not able to answer all the questions put to her, but by now the evidence was stacking up against Pugh. The inquest jury brought a verdict of wilful murder, and he was committed for trial at the Summer Assizes. There he was found guilty and sentenced to death.

Pugh had acted evasively from the beginning, first trying to avoid being seen by Hitchcock and others, then denying that he had visited the farm, only to contradict himself later on. He had also failed to cover his tracks, leaving spots and stains of blood on his exit from the barn, and carrying them on his clothing. In addition to the graze mark on his forehead, more scratches were found on his ears and hand, suggesting that Lizzie had clawed him with her nails before being killed. When the Wilsons came forward to testify over the discarded shirt, he had no hope of a reprieve. William Pugh went to his execution at Derby Gaol on Wednesday 5 August 1896, having partaken of Holy Communion and passed the time after breakfast by singing hymns. Once he left the cell he did not speak, and betrayed no sign of fear. At 8.10 am Billington, the executioner, operated the drop, and Pugh plunged downwards to an instantaneous death. Outside, an enormous crowd of the usual 'ghouls' awaited the raising of the black flag, which indicated that the hanging had taken place.

Mystery still lingers as to Pugh's reason for killing Lizzie Boot. Granted, her adverse comments about his courtship of Sarah Saunders must have rankled with him, but to repay unkind words by butchery with a billhook seems rather drastic. One cannot help feeling there is more going on here than meets the eye. When Pugh eventually made his confession, he claimed that his motive was robbery. He knew Lizzie had money, and had promised to take Sarah on a trip to Alfreton. He murdered his victim in an effort to obtain the funds. Again, this may have been true, but had Pugh told all? A loving son, he had parted from his mother in an emotional scene at the trial, and may well have not wished to distress her with further revelations. The murder itself does not have the hallmarks of a cold-blooded, premeditated plan, but shows the reckless fury of a crime of passion. It is as if Pugh was past caring, and snatched up the nearest lethal weapon to strike savagely and blindly, heedless of the consequences. Afterwards, his clumsy efforts at concealment were doomed to failure.

Why did Lizzie go to the barn with Pugh? Was it to avoid a scene in front of her young niece? Had Pugh been one of the several suitors rejected in the past? Or is it possible that Lizzie had once been smitten by him, and therefore resented his courtship of Sarah? Certainly he had been seen hanging around Lindway Farm in the past, accompanying Mr Limb as the farmer ploughed, and running errands for others. One

Lindway Lane and Farm, Brackenfield, the scene of the murder. Ann Krawszik

suspects that he was more likely to have taken an interest in the pretty housekeeper than in her employer. Given Pugh's 'jack-the-lad' persona, he may well have thought he could charm Lizzie into giving him money, and maybe even something else. When his overtures were repulsed, he reacted with terrible violence. But now we are well into the realms of speculation, and the only honest answer is that we may never know.

Whatever the reason, Lizzie Boot did not deserve to die so brutally at such an early age. William Pugh struck the two fatal blows, and by so doing condemned himself to death. Two young lives were effectively ended by the billhook in the barn.

CHAPTER 10

Illicit Love
1902

oseph Price was an unlucky man. Years ago, as a miner at Hartington colliery, he had suffered crippling injuries in a pit accident that rendered him unable to work. As if this were not enough, at a later date he was knocked down on the Great Central Railway line, and suffered further injuries. Some might say he was lucky to still be alive, but Price might not have agreed with them. An unemployable cripple, he had for several years relied on his wife Nancy to be the family breadwinner. And Nancy, a robust, healthy woman in her forties, had needs of another kind that apparently he could no longer meet.

For the past thirteen years, the Prices had been on friendly terms with John Bedford, a labourer at the coke ovens of the Grassmoor Colliery Company. He often came out to visit them at their cottage, Oxpasture, on Parker's Lane in the village of Duckmanton. Bedford seemed especially fond of Nancy, who at forty-eight was seven years older than her admirer. In order to earn income for herself and her husband, she kept a fried fish shop on the outskirts of Calow, near to the Arkwright Town bridge, and spent a fair amount of time away from home, and from Joseph. The shop was not far from the

White Hart Inn, *Calow, where Nancy Price drank for the last time.* Dennis

Prices' cottage, but it was even closer to the *White Hart Inn* at Calow, and Nancy and Bedford had often been known to go drinking there together. Joseph had noticed Bedford's affectionate attitude towards his wife, but put it down to their long-standing friendship, and was not aware of anything untoward.

In fact, by 1902 John and Nancy had been lovers for a decade and more, and were seen openly displaying their feelings in public on more than one occasion. Joseph Price often travelled into Chesterfield to visit friends and stay overnight, and on these regular journeys Bedford would join Nancy at the cottage for a night of love. Theirs was a passionate relationship, which had evidently satisfied their needs for many years. The downside was that it seemed to bring out the worst in Bedford's nature. A pale, moustached man, otherwise quiet and respectable in his behaviour, Bedford was known to friends for his jealous rages, and over the years he had grown very possessive of his mistress. There had been quarrels, and in May 1902 Bedford had used such bad language during an argument at the cottage that Mr Price had ordered him to leave. In spite of this, Bedford and Nancy always made up afterwards, and there seemed no reason to think that their illicit liaison would not continue. Unfortunately for this arrangement, a third person entered the equation. At some point a younger man, whose name was never revealed and who was apparently unknown to the police, made the acquaintance of Nancy Price, who was evidently flattered by his attentions. Just how far this new friendship went is open to debate, but it is clear that Bedford suspected the worst, and began to plot revenge.

At 10 pm on Wednesday 25 June 1902, John Bedford and Nancy Price were drinking at the *White Hart*, seemingly happy in each other's company. Joseph Price had gone to Chesterfield, and was staying the night at his brother-in-law's house, leaving the former lovers to themselves. After a while Nancy left the inn and went home, leaving Bedford drinking inside. When he came out, he looked around for her, and asked a man standing outside which way she had gone. Obviously, Nancy had not arranged to meet him afterwards.

The man replied that she had gone 'down the lane' towards her cottage, and Bedford then took the same route. Neither of them was seen again that night.

The following morning, at 6.45, John Bedford arrived once more at the *White Hart*, and had a glass of beer. In spite of the early hour, unusual for him, there were other drinkers present, and the talk for some reason came round to changing trousers. Bedford remarked that the pair he was wearing would be 'neither good to me nor thee before long'. Asked why this was so, he replied that they would see. He then left the inn.

Shortly after 9 am he called to a man named Fred Wagstaffe outside the *White Hart*, and told him he had killed Nancy Price. When Wagstaffe, a close friend, refused to believe him, Bedford showed his trouser legs and boots, which were splashed with blood. This shocking revelation upset Wagstaffe so much he started to cry, at which Bedford offered to take him to the cottage and show him the body. He had locked it up inside, he claimed, and showed the house key as proof. He told the same story to a group of drinkers outside the pub, but they told him to shut up, thinking he was talking nonsense. The Bedford they knew was a quiet, inoffensive character, certainly no murderer. Wagstaffe and Bedford set off for Oxpasture, and were joined on the way by Robert Davidson. Wagstaffe was glad of his company, as he had begun to be scared of what lay ahead.

At the cottage Bedford unlocked the door and showed them into the downstairs room. There they found Nancy Price lying dead on the sofa, the front of her skull battered in and spattered with blood. She had been darning a stocking when the attack began, and still held the stocking and darning needle in her lifeless hands. Blood from the violent death-blows splashed the walls and ceiling of the room, and discoloured a heap of clean white clothes on the kitchen table. The murder weapon, an eighteen-inch poker, lay nearby, thickly stained with drying blood, proof that the crime had been committed hours before. Bedford told his appalled companions that he had loved his victim, but that she had betrayed him, and now he had taken his revenge. As the three men left the cottage, he bade a passionate farewell to his dead mistress, exclaiming: 'Goodbye, darling. I have loved thee, but thou has deceived me.' Shocked

Duckmanton village, where at her home on Parker's Lane Mrs Price met her death. Dennis Middleton

at what he had seen, and thinking Bedford had gone mad, Wagstaffe offered to take his friend to see a doctor, but the latter declined. Davidson later indicated that, having killed Nancy, Bedford no longer wished to live. The three men returned to the *White Hart* and informed the licensee, Mr Harrison, who sent for the police. P C Frank Outram arrived and took Bedford into custody. By now the prisoner was showing the effects of the beer he had drunk. He readily admitted that he had 'done it', laughed as the handcuffs went on his wrists, remarking: 'This beats all your bloody Coronation', then launched into a rendition of the Boer War favourite, 'Goodbye, Dolly Gray'. A more sombre journey was that made by Joseph Price, who returned home to find his wife a corpse and their long-time friend a self-confessed murderer.

John Bedford's fate was now sealed. Jealousy over Nancy's 'infidelity', whether real or imagined, had led him to a savage act of violence against his former mistress and another man's wife. Condemned to death, he spent his last days expressing penitence and remorse for what he had done, and the day before his execution was united with his parents, brother and sisters for an emotional parting scene in his cell. He went to his death on another Wednesday, 30 July 1902, the regular executioner Billington being assisted by Henry Pierrepoint. The drop fell at 8 am, and for the first time no black flag was raised. Only the sombre tolling of the bell gave notice to the crowd outside that Nancy Price's killer had paid his final debt.

CHAPTER 11

A Razor in the Manger
1903

S amuel Parker was a well known figure in North Derbyshire. Vice-Chairman of the Chesterfield Board of Guardians, he lived outside the town at Hill Top Farm, Temple Normanton, a village to the south of Chesterfield itself. Under his ownership the farm had prospered, and Mr Parker and his wife clearly felt that some of its success was owing to the excellent servants they had. In particular, young Frances Rawson won their unstinting praise. The sixteen-year-old daughter of the widow Charlotte Rawson, whose family lived at Nicholas Street in Hasland, Frances had been with them for just over a year. The Parkers were pleased with her work, and often reflected that they 'had never had so good a servant'.

Nicholas Street, Hasland, home of murder victim Frances Rawson. Dennis Middleton

An employee of a different kind was Samuel Redfern. At twenty-five he was nine years older than Frances. Redfern originated from Ashleyhay, and had worked as a wagoner for Mr Parker since November 1902, his father having been a servant at Hill Farm thirty years before. When he first started, the Parkers had found his heavy drinking caused them problems, but for the last few months he had managed to abstain from alcohol. Redfern was a steady worker, but where Frances was noted for her pleasant, sunny disposition, the wagoner was a quiet, moody loner whose sullen temperament did not endear him to his fellow labourers. He had made no friends at the farm, and with one exception kept himself to himself.

The exception was Frances Rawson.

For some time now it had become obvious to everyone else at Hill Farm that Redfern was smitten with Frances. Mr Parker himself often noticed how he would leave whatever he was doing and follow the young girl wherever she went, offering to help her chop the kindling she gathered for the fire and assisting her with various other tasks. Other farm labourers would later testify that he often asked them if Frances went anywhere, or met anyone in her free time. There was nothing they could tell him, as there was no indication that Frances was courting, or had a regular young man, but Redfern remained sulky and suspicious, unsatisfied with their answers.

On a weekend visit to her mother at Nicholas Street, Frances told the widow that on 26 August, during the Hasland Flower Show, Sam Redfern had asked her to go out with him. The teenager had given him short shrift, telling him he should be ashamed of himself, asking a girl like herself out, when he was 'old enough to be her father'! To Frances at least, Redfern must have seemed much older than his twenty-five years! Almost a month later, on 24 September, Redfern had offered his unwilling beloved a silver watch chain, only to be told that the object of his affections wanted nothing from him. Mrs Rawson told her daughter to report him to the Parkers if he continued to bother her.

On Sunday 4 October, when the girl visited her mother again, Redfern invited himself along for the walk to Hasland,

and once more urged her to accept him. When he was refused, he made veiled threats about what might happen to Frances if she would not accept him. This time, though, Frances did not tell her mother.

The following Tuesday, 6 October 1903, Sam Redfern came into the farm kitchen at about 5.30 pm to get matches for lighting a fire under the copper. Soon after he had gone, Frances Rawson returned from buying stamps at the Post Office, picked up a bucket from the kitchen and set off towards the stable, intending to fetch kindling for the fire. She had only been gone ten minutes, and the Parkers were settling down for the evening, when they heard Frances come rushing back into the kitchen. Holding her bloodstained apron to her throat, the girl got almost to the sitting room, leaning on the dresser, and gasped out: 'Oh, Missus Parker – sticks – Sam!' Mrs Parker managed to catch her as she fell, lowering her to the ground. Horrified, she and her husband saw that Frances had a gash across her throat, and blood was pumping out over her clothes, spattering her employers. The poor girl died soon after.

Meanwhile, hearing the commotion, farm labourers James Laude and William Lewis went in search of Sam Redfern. They found him in the cart shed, lying face down in a pool of blood, and with two wounds on his throat. Still alive, he asked Laude if Frances was dead, and was told she was. When Laude asked the injured man why he had done it, Redfern answered that: 'it was on account of her deceiving me.' Laude found Redfern's muffler and a bloodstained razor that he knew was the wagoner's property in the manger.

The alarm was raised, and P C Allblaster arrived from Bond's Main, Dr John Buckley of Hasland following at about 7 pm. Finding poor Frances beyond help, they turned their attentions to Redfern, and managed to staunch the flow of blood. Dr Buckley stitched the main wound, and Redfern was taken to the Chesterfield Workhouse Hospital on Newbold Road, where he eventually recovered. A further search of the premises by Allblaster and P C Moorcroft on Wednesday revealed signs of a struggle in the shed, with sticks and fodder strewn about, and a grisly trail of blood leading all the way

Temple Normanton village. Not far from here, at Hilltop Farm, Frances Rawson was killed by farm worker Samuel Redfern. Dennis Middleton

from the shed to the kitchen door. Allblaster then went to the Workhouse Hospital and charged Redfern with murder.

Although not fit to attend the first day of the inquest at the *Lord's Arms*, Temple Normanton, on Thursday 8 October, Samuel Redfern was sufficiently recovered to appear there when it was resumed the following Tuesday. By then Dr Buckley was able to give the results of his post-mortem examination. Frances Rawson had died as the result of bleeding from a wound, four inches long and two inches deep, running from beneath her right ear to the middle of her throat. This had been enough to sever the right external jugular vein. There were two slight cuts on the chin, and more on the fingers of her right hand. They were of a kind that might have been dealt by the bloodstained razor, and could not have been self-inflicted. He confirmed that there had been no 'outrage' committed on the girl. The jury returned a verdict of wilful murder against Redfern, who was subsequently sentenced to death at the Derbyshire Winter Assizes.

During the trial, questions had been raised as to Redfern's sanity. It seemed that there had been mental illness in the family, and it was suggested by his defence that he might be suffering from the same problems. Certainly, his claim that he killed Frances because she 'deceived' him, and that he had seen her with her boyfriend, who later threatened him, seem to have had no basis other than in his own troubled imagination. John Booker, the girl's uncle, who identified the body, had seen Frances during her visit to Hasland on the Sunday prior to the murder, and Redfern may have mistaken him for a non-existent lover. At any rate, his defence felt their case was strong enough to lodge an appeal against the death sentence on the grounds of insanity.

Following an examination by two Home Office Commissioners, who were startled to find that his mental development was less than that of a nineteen-year-old, the Home Secretary notified Derby Gaol on 14 December that the killer of Frances Rawson was to be 'respited' from the capital offence. Samuel Redfern escaped the rope and instead served life imprisonment for manslaughter. Apparently he received the good news, as he had listened to the death sentence, with the same impassive calm.

CHAPTER 12

Innocent Lives
1904

To their neighbours on High Street, the Bowmans seemed an ideal family. The young couple and their two pretty little daughters had moved to Mosborough from Whittington Moor two or three years ago, and since then had established themselves as popular members of the community in the mining village that lay close to North-east Derbyshire's border with South Yorkshire. Joseph Henry Bowman worked as manager of the Mosborough branch of Messrs Wright & Sons, provision dealers, of Whittington Moor. His short, cheerful figure was a familiar and welcome sight to his customers, as was his two-year-old daughter Martha, who regularly played in front of the shop.

Mr Bowman had worked for Wrights in Whittington Moor from the age of twelve, and nothing but good was spoken of him and his wife by those who had known them. A conscientious worker, he had also been a useful footballer with the Whittington Moor Tradesmen's team, and a regular attender at the Congregational Church, although this last may have owed something to the fact that Martha Barrett, his future wife, sang contralto in the choir! Always courteous and well-behaved, he was regarded by his High Street neighbours as the perfect husband and father, and blessed with a

High Street, Mosborough, scene of the Bowman family tragedy in 1904. Dennis Middleton

family to match. Sadly for all concerned, Joseph Bowman's domestic happiness was overlain by the shadow of guilt that would, in time, prove destructive to himself and those dearest to him.

On Sunday morning, 8 May 1904, a letter arrived for Mr Bowman from his employers, informing him that stock-taking was to take place at the Mosborough premises the following morning. The date chosen was three weeks earlier than expected, nothing sinister in itself, but evidently it had a profound effect on the man who read it. Although Bowman behaved normally for the rest of the day, the dark seeds of violence had been sown in his mind.

No outward sign appeared in the behaviour of the family that day. Bowman took little Martha for a walk, and he and his wife treated each other with obvious affection. That evening, he helped her get Martha and fourteen-month-old Charlotte ready for bed, afterwards reading a newspaper beside the older child's cradle as Mrs Bowman carried out various household tasks. The couple ate supper together and cleared away, making their own way upstairs for the night. During the night they were awoken twice by one of the little girls, and each time Bowman got out of bed and soothed the child to sleep again. Eventually Mrs Bowman, too, fell asleep.

She awoke suddenly, at around 4.45 am, as someone or something struck her a violent blow on the back of the head. Shocked and badly hurt, she struggled to get up, only to be hit again, the blow this time striking her temple. By now Mrs Bowman realised that she was being attacked by her own husband, but in spite of the obvious danger she was in, her first thought was for the girls. She was heard to scream out: 'Oh, my children! My children!'

Her cries were heard by her next door neighbours, the Laughtons, who kept a cycle shop adjoining the Bowman's premises. Mrs Laughton, thinking the children must be ill, urged her husband to go and see what was wrong. While getting dressed, Mr Laughton heard more screams, and looked out of the window to see Mrs Bowman standing in the yard, clad only in her nightdress and covered in blood.

Laughton rushed downstairs. Gilbert Keeton was outside,

ready to go to work. Hearing the noise, he also made towards the shop. When he got there, Keeton, who knew Mrs Bowman, was horrified at the sight of a woman pouring blood from head wounds, and so badly marked by the blows that at first he did not recognise her. Gradually realising that this was Martha Bowman, he asked who had done this to her, and the distraught mother told him: 'It is Joe, but never mind me; look to my children.'

Mrs Bowman, now close to collapse, was taken in by another neighbour, Mrs Staton. Meanwhile Laughton and Keeton had been joined by Postmaster Kemp and Harry Stones, and the four men dashed into the house. In the kitchen they found spots of blood left by the fleeing woman, and guessed that Bowman and the children must be upstairs. Keeton, who thought the shopkeeper might have fired a gun at his wife, grabbed the kitchen poker and led the rush upstairs. No-one answered their calls, but a gurgling noise could be heard from the bedroom. The door was locked, and Keeton took a running kick at it, repeating the action until it gave way.

They burst in to find a nightmare scene. Charlotte, the younger child, lolled across the bed, her skull smashed by violent blows. Her sister Martha lay in her cot, her throat viciously gashed across from ear to ear, but incredibly still breathing. In desperation, Kemp tied clothing round the wound, but the poor girl lived for less than a quarter of an hour. Gilbert Keeton carried the baby, Charlotte, out to the kitchen and laid her on a couch, hoping to revive her, but saw at once that she was beyond all help.

Joseph Bowman lay in a pool of blood on the carpet at the foot of the bed. More blood poured from several deep wounds across his throat. Nearby lay the two murder weapons, an open razor and heavy iron pipe tongs, which Bowman had borrowed not long before to tighten a nut on a pipe in the house. Both were coated and splashed with blood.

By now the authorities had been alerted, and P C Bennett came to the house, followed soon after by Dr A McLaren Pilcher. The doctor quickly established that Charlotte was already dead, and attempted to save Martha, but his efforts were in vain. Turning his attention to Mrs Bowman, Pilcher

stitched a half-inch wound at the back of her head and a second injury to the side of the forehead above the eye, which had cut the flesh to the bone. He then had the badly injured Bowman removed to Sheffield Hospital for treatment. There, the murderer spoke for the first time since being found in the bedroom, telling Laughton that he knew he had done wrong. Laughton asked if money was the problem, and was told it was, and had been going on for some time. Chillingly, Bowman added: 'I wanted to leave no offspring behind me.' After this outburst his condition deteriorated rapidly, and his last words to Laughton were: 'She's been a good wife to me.' Joseph Henry Bowman died between 10 and 11 am on Monday 9 May 1904, of his self-inflicted wounds. He was twenty-six.

The subsequent inquests on father and daughters revealed that money had indeed been the problem. Bowman had told his wife that trade was bad, and had indulged in minor betting with the firm's funds to help improve matters. If he had indeed been doing this for as long as he suggested to Laughton, he must have won most of his bets, as the books had been inspected and found to be correct up to a week before the murders. At this point, however, he had found himself £17 short, and the unexpected news of the forthcoming stock-taking had made him panic, with terrible results.

Friends who were witnesses at the inquest made a point of saying that they would willingly have loaned him such a small sum, had they known of his trouble, but they also admitted that for a man like Bowman the disgrace of having to explain himself would have been too much to bear. Rather than humiliate himself, he had taken the lives of his innocent daughters and attempted to kill his wife, before ending his own life.

P C Walker found a note by the bed, written by Bowman to

his father-in-law, Mr A Barrett, which confirmed the statements of the witnesses. Joseph Bowman confessed that he had speculated Wrights' money, and incurred a £17 debt. He informed Barrett that the family were all insured with the Wesleyan Insurance Society, and urged his father-in-law to pay off the debt to the firm.

Mrs Martha Bowman, the sole and wretched survivor of this dreadful family tragedy, returned to her father's house in Sanforth Street to keep her away from the frenzy of reporters and local gossip as she gradually recovered from her injuries. It was to Sanforth Street, too, that the coffins carrying the bodies of her husband and two little daughters came, on their way for burial at Newbold parish church. Large crowds viewed their arrival, and lined the streets to the Newbold churchyard, and the *Derbyshire Times* was to report that the funeral was followed by thousands of people. They came not only from Mosborough and Whittington Moor, but from all over north Derbyshire to pay their respects. It was as if they too were a part of the sad events of Monday 9 May 1904, that had so brutally claimed two innocent young lives.

Below: *St John's Church, Newbold.* Ann Krawszik
Right: *Newbold churchyard, where the two Bowman girls were laid to rest.* Ann Krawszik

CHAPTER 13

As Good a Son as a Mother Ever Reared
1905

S ometimes good soldiers make bad civilians. Reined in by tough Army discipline and sustained by the fellowship of their comrades, some have been known to find it hard to accustom themselves to a life out of uniform. The terrible example set by Alfred Gough in Brimington in 1881 was followed in the 1900s, when Chesterfield suffered three savage murders in the space of eighteen months. All were committed by former serving soldiers, and the first of them took place in Spa Lane in August 1905.

John Silk had joined the 5th Irish Lancers in 1894, and had served abroad in India, and in South Africa during the Boer

Spa Lane, view east from St Mary's Gate. Here in 1905 John Silk murdered his mother Mary Fallon in a drunken rage. Ann Krawszik

War. His military superiors were fully satisfied with his conduct while in uniform, but after leaving the Army in 1903, Silk's behaviour had grown more unpredictable. He had begun to drink heavily while on military service, and when he took up a labouring job in Chesterfield the habit continued.

Friends and acquaintances came to regard him as something of a Jekyll and Hyde character, amiable and good-natured when sober, but given to violent outbursts when 'in drink'. This behaviour seemed especially marked in his relations with his mother, Mrs Mary Fallon, with whom Silk and their lodger Thomas Meakin shared a home at No 3 Spa Lane. John Canavan, Silk's uncle and the brother of Mrs Fallon, lived nearby at No 1 on the same street. Spa Lane, a back road running off St Mary's Gate and linking with Station Road and Station Back Lane, is now familiar to most as the location of a car park, but in Edwardian days it was described as 'a low neighbourhood', one of the seedier areas of town, where acts of vice and drunken violence were commonplace events.

Mary Fallon has to be regarded as a singularly unlucky woman. Three times married, her first and second husbands had both died prematurely, and the third and last, the collier Edward Fallon, had deserted her. As if this were not bad enough, Mary was crippled with rheumatism and sciatica, with one leg badly bent and drawn up. She moved around with the help of crutches, and had recently been carried from place to place on a chair. Silk, the son of her first husband, was normally very fond of his mother and did his best to look after her. On those occasions he was drunk, however, he and Mary were liable to quarrel violently. Thomas Meakin, the lodger, had seen Silk strike his mother when he had had too much to drink. He was later to claim that, when he intervened to stop the young ex-soldier hurting the crippled woman, Mary had 'not thanked him' for his interference.

On the evening of Saturday 5 August 1905, John Silk went out on one of his weekend drinking binges. He was seen by several witnesses at 8 pm and afterwards, in a drunken and abusive state. He was also heard to make ominous threats that 'there would be a murder in Spa Lane tonight', and that the victim would be 'our old girl'. John Canavan, his uncle and the brother of Mary Fallon, encountered his nephew twice that night, at 8 and later at 9.35 pm. Seeing that Silk was the worse for drink, and likely to get himself into trouble, he advised the young man to go home.

It appears that Silk returned to the house twice during the evening, each time quarrelling with his mother, before going out to drink again. On the second occasion, at 10.15, a teenage neighbour, Ruth Allsopp, went to the house and found Silk and his mother there.

As Silk left for another visit to the public house, Mary handed a bottle to him and asked him to get her a half noggin of whisky. He responded by hurling the bottle to the ground, where it smashed to pieces, and then picking up chunks of broken glass and throwing them at her.

It was 11.15 pm by the time he came back again, very much the worse for wear. This time he was brought home by Henry Goodwin, who had decided Silk was in too bad a state to wander home alone. Arriving at No 3 Spa Lane, Goodwin pushed Silk in through the door, and stayed only a short time before leaving. When Silk entered the house, he saw his mother seated on the sofa by the kitchen table, reading a newspaper, and Thomas Meakin sitting nearby, having returned an hour or so before. The paraffin lamp on the table gave only a feeble light, and Silk reached out and began to turn it up. Mary Fallon told him to leave it alone, and reached out to push it away from him. This was all the provocation John Silk needed, and he exploded into murderous action.

Silk slapped his mother on both sides of the face, and grabbed at her, his weight sending the table over as he lunged forward. The lamp crashed to the floor and smashed, and the room was plunged into darkness. Meakin, getting up, heard the noise of violent scuffling on the ground, and the voice of Mrs Fallon crying out: 'Oh, John! Don't!' This was followed by the sound of kicks and blows, and Mrs Fallon screaming 'Murder!' and 'Police!' Bearing in mind her attitude the last time he had tried to part them, Meakin hurried out to find a policeman.

Mrs Emma Watson, who lived nearby at No 1 Hall's Court, heard the groaning of Mary Fallon as she was attacked. She saw Meakin come out of the house, obviously agitated and wringing his hands. He asked her to go and fetch a policeman,

Spital Cemetery, where Dr Green conducted the inquest on Mary Fallon. Ann Krawszik

but Mrs Watson, unwilling to get involved, told him to go and find one himself. At this point John Silk appeared in the doorway behind them, and called out menacingly to the frightened Meakin: 'Oh, you'll find a policeman, will you, you bugger?' He then went back inside and locked the door.

Meakin went across to James Kelly's house at No 11 Spa Lane, and told him there was 'a bit of bother on'. When asked what he meant, he replied that Silk was ill-using his mother, and 'he is kicking her, he has kicked her right under the sofa.' Kelly was not keen to interfere either; he was later to claim in court that he was 'not a strong man' and receiving medical attention. He certainly did not relish an encounter with the drunken, belligerent Silk. Seeing that Meakin had donned neither coat nor cap in his hurry, Kelly lent him his cap and told him to find a policeman.

Getting no help from him, Meakin went to the top of Spa Lane, where he met Sergeant Prince and told him he had better go to No 3, as there was 'a quarrel' there. The sergeant, evidently dismissing it as another minor 'domestic' incident, assured Meakin that 'it will all be all right in a few minutes.' He then walked away, the worried lodger calling after him to remember that he had reported the incident to him.

When Meakin returned, the house was locked against him, and although the fight appeared over, he thought he could hear sounds of muttering. He went to James Kelly and told him about it, and the latter offered to put him up for the night, rather than disturb Silk and his mother. Meakin agreed, and got to bed there around 1 am. He and Kelly heard nothing else that night.

At 10.50 on Sunday morning, Henry Dye called at No 3. Dye was a brewery labourer, and earned himself a little extra by delivering newspapers. When he knocked on the door, he was surprised to get no answer, and finding it unlocked, went inside. There he found Mary Fallon lying dead on her back on the hearthrug, and blood and smashed glass and pottery articles everywhere.

Dye ran out to find a policeman, and P C Frank Sykes went to the house. Taking a closer look, he saw that the crippled woman had suffered terrible bruises to the head and face, and had bled heavily from her mouth and nostrils. Blood matted her hair, and soaked the floor around her. The table had been stood upright with the lamp upon it, but smashed lamp glass littered the floor. Sykes went upstairs to the bedroom, and there found John Silk apparently asleep in bed, his back to the wall. As Sykes entered, he seemed to wake up, but when questioned, he claimed to know nothing of what had happened. Turning back the covers, Sykes saw that Silk had bloodstains on his hands and throat. He ordered the young man to get dressed.

As they came downstairs they passed an earthenware wash basin, and Silk began to wash his bloody hands, but was ordered by Sykes to stop. Holding out his bloodstained arms, he asked: 'Because of these?' He was then placed under arrest, and taken to the police station.

John Silk appeared before the Chesterfield magistrates, Dr J G Shea and Theophilus Pearson, on Monday 7 August, where he was charged with the murder of his mother. Statements were heard from Chief Constable Kilpatrick and the lodger, Thomas Meakin, and the prisoner was remanded in custody until the following morning. On Monday afternoon Dr A Green presided over an inquest at Chesterfield Cemetery, where John Canavan identified the body, and he and Meakin were among those giving evidence. Dr W J Symes, a Chesterfield surgeon, presented the results of the post-mortem he had conducted on Sunday, and which revealed the sickening nature of the attack carried out on Mary Fallon. She had sustained savage blows to the head which had severely bruised both hemispheres of the brain, and broken her nose, and her neck bore further bruising which suggested an attempt at strangulation. Most repulsive of all, violent pressure had caved in her chest, breaking four ribs – two of them broken in two places – whose jagged ends had torn into her lung, causing a massive internal haemorrhage. This, and the shock of the attack, were the cause of death.

Dr Symes agreed that the head injuries may well have been inflicted with the broken chair leg or the butt end of the bloodstained crutch, both of which were produced in court. The terrible bodily injuries were probably the result of someone jumping violently on her with both shod feet, or dropping on to her with both knees. There was no way they could have been caused by an accidental fall. The doctor had examined the clothes Silk was wearing when arrested, and had found bloodstains on the shirt and trousers. The latter also held some grey hairs that appeared to match those of the dead woman.

The inquest was adjourned to the following day, when more witnesses gave evidence, none of which was any help to John Silk. His drunken threats had been overheard, and his previous violence was well known. Meakin and Canavan, who testified to his good character when sober, were forced to admit that he was a different man after a few drinks.

Canavan's description of Silk – 'as good a son as a mother ever reared' – was qualified by the comment that when drunk 'he was the same as if he wasn't altogether right.' Meakin also admitted that he had been told how Silk 'went off his head when drunk'. Canavan's view, that the malaria and enteric fever his nephew had suffered in the Army had changed his character, does not appear to have weighed heavily with the inquest jury, and they returned a murder verdict.

After several delays due to the unavailability of witnesses, John Silk stood trial for murder at the Derbyshire Winter Assizes on 5 December 1905. Standing in court in erect, soldierly fashion, he pleaded 'not guilty' to the charge, but his cause was already lost. The jury rejected the plea of his Defence for manslaughter, and returned the same grim verdict, and Mr Justice Bucknill donned the black cap to pass sentence. As Silk left the dock, a lone friendly voice called out to him: 'Goodbye, John.' Attempts to win a reprieve were rejected on 27 December, and two days later, at the usual time of 8 am on 29 December 1905, John Silk made his final rendezvous with the hangman. He was twenty-nine years old.

The atrocious nature of the murder of a mother by her own son, and his apparent callous behaviour afterwards, shocked the whole of Chesterfield. The most recent previous murder, of Nancy Price by John Bedford, had been outside the town at Calow, and Chesterfield had begun to pride itself on the fact that no such crime had blighted them for almost twenty years since William Goddard's brutal killing of his wife on Station Lane. Now the town struggled to comprehend the horror of what had taken place on Saturday 5 August, only yards from that death in 1882. And worse was to follow very soon.

CHAPTER 14

A Razor's Edge
1906

When Walter Marsh finally left the Army, he could look back on seventeen years of distinguished service. As a member of the Staffordshire Regiment he had fought for his country in India, the Sudan, and against the Boers in South Africa. During his career he had been awarded the Silver Star and the Khedive's Medal for his conduct at the battle of Omdurman against the Mahdi's forces, the King's Medal and the Queen's Medal with clasps for his bravery in South Africa. Marsh ended his military service with the rank of Colour-Sergeant, and the best possible conduct citation – 'very good' – on his record. This, though, was less than the full story. It was later to become clear that Marsh had a fierce temper which he was not always able to control, and that his violent outbursts had got him into trouble while still in uniform. According to one soldier who had known him, one group of recruits hated him so much they burned Sergeant Marsh's bunk! While a soldier, Marsh had managed to keep his innate violence mostly within limits, but once he entered civilian life things took a decided turn for the worse.

Factory Street, Brampton, along which William Wootton ran in his stockinged feet for the police following the murder of Eliza Marsh in 1906. Dennis Middleton

In 1901, on one of his brief spells of service in England, Walter Marsh had married Eliza Gascoyne in Stafford before leaving a few months later for the South African War. Eliza hailed from Brampton, and at nineteen was considerably younger than the thirty-four-year-old Marsh.

When he left the Army in 1903, the couple moved to Sheffield in order to run a public house, funded by a substantial sum of money that Marsh had saved while a canteen sergeant in India. The business venture failed, and Marsh and Eliza came back to Brampton, where they rented a house from Edward Silcock at No 6 Goyt Terrace. Marsh, who still had a fair amount of income, does not seem to have gone out of his way to find work, preferring to live on his own means. This appears not to have met with his wife's approval, but what concerned Eliza far more was her husband's attitude towards herself.

Although the couple were parents to two young children – three-year-old Harold and baby daughter Gladys – it was clear that the marriage had long been under stress. Marsh, a tough authority figure accustomed to respect and obedience while in uniform, no doubt found it hard to adjust to civilian life with a younger wife. He soon showed himself to be fiercely jealous and possessive where Eliza was concerned, and all too ready to resort to violence. Eliza's father and sister had lived with them for a time, but both left following arguments with Marsh which stemmed from his brutal treatment of Eliza. Both George and Sophia Gascoyne had seen Marsh strike his wife, and just before Christmas 1905 the latter heard him threaten to do 'John Silk' on her, an ominous reference to the savage murder carried out in Chesterfield that year.

In May 1906 the relationship reached breaking point. Eliza left her husband and moved in with her father at No 20 Shipley Street, soon afterwards applying to the Chesterfield magistrates for a separation order on the grounds of Marsh's cruelty. Her application was turned down, the magistrates arguing that she had not been able to provide sufficient evidence, and pointing to her husband's distinguished service record. Instead, they urged a reconciliation with her husband. Marsh, having received the summons from Eliza, offered to mend his ways, and she returned to Goyt Terrace. For the space of a few weeks, there was peace in the household. Then, once again, that peace was shattered.

The houses on Goyt Terrace were new, built only two years before, and their owner was a young man named Edward Silcock. Walter Marsh, perhaps as part of his plan to win back Eliza, had recently secured a job at the Plowright Brothers' factory in Brampton, and supplemented his income by collecting rents for Silcock. On Wednesday 4 July 1906 Edward Silcock called at No 6 Goyt Terrace to see the rent books in order to fill in a return to the assistant overseer. He found that Marsh was not at home, but spoke to Eliza, who told him as many names as she could remember. At some stage in the conversation another neighbour called, and seeing Silcock there, mentioned the fact that it was Brampton Wakes, and asked him to treat them. Silcock promptly paid out a shilling for a gallon of beer.

When Marsh returned, Eliza mentioned this to him. He immediately flew into a rage at the thought of a younger man 'drinking in his house' alone with his wife, and claimed that the shilling had been paid for 'services' of another kind. Marsh stormed round to the *Bold Rodney* public house where Silcock lived, and in an abusive manner accused the landlord of improper relations with Eliza. Silcock lost his temper in return, informed Marsh that he was sacked and had better leave the house at Goyt Terrace. The enraged husband returned home with vengeance on his mind.

On Thursday 5 July, Alice Wootton, the next-door neighbour, heard what sounded like a struggle in the yard, and went over

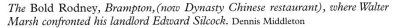

The Bold Rodney, *Brampton, (now Dynasty Chinese restaurant), where Walter Marsh confronted his landlord Edward Silcock.* Dennis Middleton

to find Marsh pinning Eliza down on the ground in the doorway, no doubt intending to harm her. Alice called out reprovingly: 'Oh, Mr Marsh!', and Marsh at once got up and let his wife go. Next day Eliza came to Alice at No 5 soaking wet, and told the neighbour that her husband had thrown water over her. Mrs Wootton, who had several times seen Eliza locked out of the house by Marsh, and once noticed what looked like a bruise on her chin, decided the young woman was safer sleeping at No 5. Eliza stayed there the next two nights, but on Sunday 8 July went back to No 6 with her husband.

That night, about 9 pm, Rose Bunting, Alice Wootton's daughter, was nursing her child at the back door of No 5, when she saw Walter Marsh pull down the window blind and heard him bolt the door. Rose then watched as Eliza unbolted the door and ran into the yard, obviously scared. She stayed there until 10 pm, when Marsh opened the door and asked her if she was coming in. Eliza replied: 'You threaten me so, Walter, I am frightened.' Marsh told her if she would not come in he would 'fetch a bobby'. He went out towards Factory Street, but came back soon afterwards, claiming that he couldn't see a policeman, but that 'Ted Silcock is at the top of the street waiting for you.'

Husband and wife went into the house, the door was locked and bolted, and Rose Bunting heard further conversation between them, with Marsh using crude expressions as he accused his wife of having illicit relations with Silcock. The next day, Monday 9 July, Marsh seemed to change completely. He apologised for his behaviour, treated Eliza kindly, and the couple were on such friendly terms it was hard to believe they had argued so fiercely the previous night. In the afternoon around 3 pm, Rose Bunting saw Marsh and Eliza, with baby Gladys in her arms, in the yard. Marsh suggested to his wife that she should take the child upstairs and 'have a sleep.' He told her he would lie down on the couch, and that he intended to go to work in the morning. He put a coin in Eliza's hand, and she informed Rose it was half a sovereign. Rose responded: 'he is good', at which Marsh told her he would give anything to his wife if she would stop telling people about their quarrels. Eliza replied that he should not 'bring other folks' names in, and accuse me of things when you know they aren't true.' The couple were still talking in friendly fashion as Rose went back inside her mother's house.

As the afternoon wore on, Marsh's temper appeared to worsen. At 5 pm he came out and complained to Rose that Eliza was 'too bloody idle' to wash the dinner pots. Shortly afterwards, he told three-year-old Harold, who was with him in the yard, to 'go upstairs to your bloody mother'. The boy obeyed, and at around 5.20 pm Rose saw Marsh walking up in the direction of Factory Street.

At 5.30 the factory hooter sounded, and soon afterwards Walter Marsh knocked at the door of No 5. On hearing that Mrs Wootton was not in, he urged Rose to 'fetch a bobby', and when she asked him why, told her: 'I've done it. I've finished her.' Seeing that Rose did not believe him, he suggested she come and see for herself. It was now that she noticed he was carrying a razor in his hand, and that there was blood on his fingers and around one wrist.

Marsh went back to No 6, and Rose followed him through the back door, which he had left open. From where she stood by the door, Rose could see the staircase door, and saw a long streak of blood around the lock. Thoroughly scared now, she shouted for her father. William Wootton came in answer, and entered the house, where Marsh told him what he had done and repeated his request for a policeman. Going upstairs, Wootton found Eliza Marsh lying on her back on the bedroom floor, her throat having been cut. Horrified, Wootton ran back downstairs and up the road to the West Ward police station, where he informed Inspector Fennemore.

Meanwhile, having already confessed to murder, Walter Marsh decided to make a run for it. This may have been an attempt to avoid 'vigilante justice' from Eliza's relatives rather than the police, but his luck was out. A neighbour had run to George Gascoyne's house crying that: 'Walter is murdering your Liza!', and he made for the house, his son John running on ahead of him. The back door of No 6 was locked, and the furious young man broke it in, eager to get at the man who had ill-treated his sister. He did not go upstairs, but on leaving by the front door saw Marsh running off along the Goyt Side. Gascoyne set off in pursuit, and eventually caught up with him in a field, knocking him to the ground.

John Ashmore, a coal agent on Factory Street, had hurried to Goyt Terrace after seeing William Wootton running to the police station in his stockinged feet. Ashmore got to the field in time to see Gascoyne 'giving Marsh some fist', and together they overpowered the killer and led him back for the police station. Before getting there they were met by Wootton and Inspector Fennemore, and the latter took Marsh into custody. It was an ignominious episode for the ex-soldier, who confirmed that he had indeed murdered his wife, told Fennemore that the razor he had used was one of a pair, and could be found in the front room, and added that he had been coming to give himself up. Earlier, he had complained to Ashmore that his wife had not made him a dinner since the previous Wednesday, but now told Fennemore that the real motive for the murder had been Eliza's 'drinking with a man called Silcock' the week before, and that since then he 'had meant to do it'. He also indicated the bloodstains on his shirt. Marsh, who was evidently still not short of money, was found to be carrying £100 in five-pound notes, two South African Kruger sovereigns, and several watches and rings.

By this time the neighbourhood had heard of the murder, and several went to the house. Edward Silcock went upstairs, found baby Gladys unharmed, and carried her outside. The police had to keep George Gascoyne in particular from attacking the prisoner, the bereaved father shouting: 'Wait till I get howd of thee!' He was prevented from carrying out his threat.

Dr James Anderson Goodfellow arrived to examine the body. At the inquest, which took place on Tuesday 10 July at Spital Cemetery, he was able to give full details of what he

Goyt Side Terrace, home of Walter and Eliza Marsh at the time of her murder.
Dennis Middleton

found. Eliza Marsh had lain on the floor beyond the foot of the bed, a pool of blood near her head, which faced away from the window. There were two wounds on her neck, the first having severed a superficial vein only. Across the front of the throat and round to the right side was the death-wound, six and a half inches long and very deep. It had severed the windpipe and carotid artery and penetrated to the spinal column, nearly cutting the head from Eliza's body. The dead woman was partly clothed, the bed had clearly been slept in, and there were further bloodstains in the middle of the pillow at neck or shoulder level, as well as spattering on the floor and furniture. Goodfellow deduced that the first wound had been inflicted while Eliza lay on the bed, and that she had suffered the second, fatal blow while on the bedroom floor. Predictably, the inquest jury gave a verdict of wilful murder on Walter Marsh.

After several appearances before the Chesterfield magistrates, Marsh came to trial at the Derbyshire Winter Assizes on 5 December 1906, a year to the day that John Silk had appeared in that court on the same charge. Amazingly, he pleaded not guilty, claiming that he had struck his wife in self-defence after she threw a glass 'lustre' ornament at him during one of their arguments. A broken glass ornament was indeed found in the bedroom, and Marsh did have bruises on his head, but the manner of Eliza's death as indicated by Dr Goodfellow argued otherwise.

Marsh's Defence Counsel spoke movingly of his splendid military record, and witnesses (mainly relatives of Marsh) were found who testified that Eliza had been lazy and uninterested in house work, but their efforts were all to no avail. The murder verdict was a foregone conclusion, and sentence was passed by the judge, Mr Justice Ridley.

Walter Marsh stood to hear it with soldierly calm, turning as if on parade to return to his cell.

An application for reprieve was suggested, but Marsh refused, apparently preferring death to a life behind bars. He was hanged at 8 am at Derby Gaol on Thursday 27 December 1906, at the age of thirty-nine. A year after being rocked by the brutal murder of Mary Fallon, Chesterfield found itself struggling to cope with an equally horrifying death. Nor was it over yet.

CHAPTER 15

The Axeman on Highfield Road
1907

Willliam Edward Slack was evidently a man of many talents, and in his time had set his hand to a variety of jobs without settling on any one of them. Apprenticed as a fitter and turner with Oliver's foundry, he suffered from the excessive noise in the workshop, and was eventually sacked after falling out with the foreman.

Slack, who seems to have been something of an athlete, then ran a gymnastics class, before teaching the science of boxing and wrestling to would-be grapplers and pugilists in the town. For a while he was hired by a local circus as an acrobat, where his displays apparently proved very popular with the audiences. Slack, though, had ambitions to become a wood-carver, and when these were thwarted he joined the Army. As a member of the Royal Marine Artillery he served a total of twelve years, including some time in India. Regarded as a good soldier, he nevertheless had a hot temper that had been known to get him into trouble. It was to prove a fatal burden to him later on.

Once out of the Army, Slack, like the Chesterfield killers of the two previous years, found it hard to get used to civilian life. He and his wife Elizabeth were partners in a childless and troubled marriage, whose problems seem

Victoria Centre, Knifesmithgate, formerly the Victoria Foundry of Messrs Oliver and Co, where William Slack was once employed. Dennis Middleton

to have been largely due to Slack himself. Like John Silk, he was described as being kind and rather quiet when sober, but made a coarse, violent drunk, and in their life together Mrs Slack had often experienced the less pleasant side of his character. Several times she had left him, only being persuaded to return by his promises to turn over a new leaf. In 1898, during one such time of separation, Slack had launched an unprovoked attack on P C Hudson of Brimington. For some reason he believed the officer knew where his wife was living, and was keeping the information from him. The assault on Hudson, where Slack had inflicted wounds with two knives he was carrying, had earned him seven years in prison.

By 1905 Slack was back in the community, working as a painter in Chesterfield for the firm of Robert Eyre and Son. In that year he took part in the repainting and decorating of the Theatre Royal on Corporation Street, where his wife Elizabeth worked as a cleaner. While engaged in this work, he met up with a former acquaintance, Lucy Wilson. Lucy, whose husband George was the caretaker and ticket-checker at the theatre, worked as a cleaner alongside Mrs Slack. She was said to have known Slack many years ago, and it was claimed by some that they were childhood sweethearts. Whether or not this was true, William Slack and Lucy Wilson certainly renewed their acquaintance at the Theatre Royal, and this was not the only time they would be seen together.

From this point the story must be approached with caution, as Slack is the narrator, and his account was written when

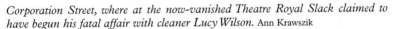

Corporation Street, where at the now-vanished Theatre Royal Slack claimed to have begun his fatal affair with cleaner Lucy Wilson. Ann Krawszik

Lucy was no longer in a position to defend herself against his accusations.

According to Slack's version of events, he and Lucy embarked on a passionate affair soon after their meeting at the theatre, and for the better part of two years arranged secret encounters in various parts of Chesterfield. Slack also claimed that the two of them made love at Lucy's home while her husband was in the house, and that her baby son Harold – born during this time – was in fact Slack's child.

The trouble started when Lucy grew tired of the undercover nature of the affair. If Slack is to be believed, she told him she was bored with Chesterfield, and urged him to run away with her and begin a new life elsewhere.

By this time the passionate lover began to get cold feet, the more so as he and Lucy had been seen together by several people. Gossip had been getting back to his wife, and one woman had threatened to tell George Wilson what was going on.

Slack tried to end the affair, but Lucy was not in a mood to let go. Slack began to feel trapped, and thoughts of murder may well have crossed his mind at this point. Certainly he started to grind the blade of a hatchet he had acquired in Chesterfield Market, and to carry it about with him, as he had previously armed himself with knives to attack P C Hudson.

On Monday 18 March 1907, Slack was working on a house at Avondale Road, in the Stonegravels area of Chesterfield. He was to claim that Lucy, still determined to make him run away with her, had threatened to come to confront him at work. William Henry Madin, a fellow workman, later testified that

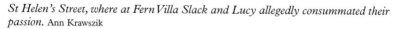

St Helen's Street, where at Fern Villa Slack and Lucy allegedly consummated their passion. Ann Krawszik

Slack explained that he was going to leave work early that lunch-time to collect thirty-five shillings he was owed, and had to go to Eastwood's Wagon Works on Brimington Road to collect it. He would make up the time later on. Slack left at 11.45 am, fifteen minutes earlier than usual, and returned a few minutes after 1 pm. When Madin asked if he had the money, Slack said that a woman would be bringing it up later that afternoon. He asked his workmate to look out for a black-clad woman in a large black hat, pushing a baby in a bassinette, in case he missed her while he was working at the back of the house.

At around 3.30 pm a woman fitting the description came to the house, and Slack went down to meet her. Madin saw the two of them engage in an animated conversation that lasted some twenty minutes, during which Slack two or three times made as if to leave, but was called back and detained by the woman, who was 'working her hands, as if excited'. She eventually left, wheeling the baby in its bassinette down Newbold Road towards the town centre, and Slack returned to work. Thirty-five minutes later he asked another workmate to finish painting a window for him, and set off the way the woman had gone.

At 5 pm a postman, James Gordon Bennett, was delivering letters along Highfield Road, only a short distance from the house on Avondale Road, where Slack had been working. As he neared the house of Isaac Eyre, he saw a man and woman, the

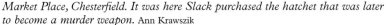

Market Place, Chesterfield. It was here Slack purchased the hatchet that was later to become a murder weapon. Ann Krawszik

latter tending a large baby carriage, were deep in conversation, although Bennett was not aware they were arguing. He had to step into the road to get round the bassinette.

He had gone twenty yards when he heard 'a noise of chopping', and turned to see the woman lying facedown on the ground, and the man aiming a vicious blow at her head with a hatchet. He must have hit her five or six times, even as Bennett was turning to look. Appalled at the sight, Bennett saw the man stand in the middle of the road grasping his blood-stained hatchet as blood poured from the head of his victim and along the gutter.

Seeing Tom Wright, the groom to Dr Worthington, working nearby, Bennett called him over and they went towards the man. Slack, for it was he, threw the hatchet into a garden, and told them: 'There's the hatchet. I'm going to give myself up. She's fetched me from work this afternoon.'

Wright kept an eye on him, while Bennett took a closer look at the woman, and found she was dead. Ever the slave to duty, even in these circumstances, the postman explained that he had to complete his round, and asked Wright if he could handle Slack alone, but the groom assured him he would manage. Bennett set off again, while Wright, noticing the baby carriage, asked what his prisoner was going to do with it. Slack told him it was his wife and child, and he would bring it along. He went back to Lucy's lifeless body, and bent to kiss her lips, afterwards kissing the baby. This was seen by Bennett as he moved away.

Wright and Slack, the latter still in his painter's white jacket and apron and wheeling the pram, set off for the police station. Before reaching it, they were met by a constable and soon after by Sergeant Fisher. Slack was taken into custody, the body of Lucy Wilson removed from the street, and the murder weapon recovered from where it had been flung into the garden.

In the mortuary, Dr Sidney Worthington examined the dead woman, and found that death had been caused by a wound to the neck that had cut through the carotid artery and interior jugular vein to reach the spine. A second blow on the back of the neck had also penetrated to the spinal column, while the fractured skull showed four separate wounds, partly exposing the brain.

Avondale Road, Chesterfield, where Slack was working as a painter and the scene of his quarrel with Lucy Wilson. Dennis Middleton

There could be no doubt as to the murderer's identity. Apart from the eyewitness testimony of Bennett and Wright, black hairs on the hatchet clearly linked it to the victim, and Slack himself admitted ownership of the weapon. Madin, his workmate, had not seen the hatchet in his possession, but knew Slack owned one, as he had once asked Madin for the loan of his whetstone to sharpen it. In any case, Slack admitted to the killing, but denied murder, claiming it was not premeditated and that he had only intended to frighten Lucy off. Unconvinced, the inquest jury and the magistrates' court returned verdicts of wilful murder, and Slack went to trial at the Assizes at the Shire Hall, Derby, on 25 June 1907.

There, Slack's defence put the case for a verdict of manslaughter, claiming that he had been provoked into killing Lucy Wilson. Clara Ford, the prisoner's sister, also testified that her brother had suffered sunstroke while on service in India, and that his behaviour had subsequently altered. Certainly Slack tended to get carried away in conversation, jabbering his words, rambling and repeating himself, and his testimony at Derby was given in such a way. He reiterated his claims that Lucy had been his mistress and the mother of his child, and that they had slept together from the night of their first meeting at the Theatre Royal. According to him, Lucy had told him that her husband, George Wilson, went with other women, and 'had not given her a farthing for seven years'. She intended to go with other men, and told Slack she didn't think much of his wife, who she felt was to blame for his earlier prison sentence, having given evidence against him.

They had met on Sunday 17 March, at 'Fern Villa', No 66 St Helen's Street, an empty house to which he had the key. Lucy had pressured Slack, forcing him to agree to meet her at the theatre the next day and come to 'a thorough understanding' about their future. He had gone there at 12.30 pm on the day of the killing, hence his excuse to leave work early, and this time Lucy had urged him to go with her to Coventry.

When he tried to get out of it, pleading that he had work to complete, he only succeeded in making her angry. She had turned up at Avondale Road and an argument had ensued, during which Lucy had threatened to drown herself and young Harold in the Brockwell Brook at the Donkey Racecourse, a favourite venue for suicides, if Slack did not agree to her demands. The argument had continued on to Highfield Road, where Lucy had grown more insulting and abusive, telling him to 'look at your bastard', and referring to his wife as a whore. Slack's temper had boiled over, and he had struck out in a furious rage, killing her. As to his carrying of the hatchet in his painter's apron, his story was that he had intended to borrow a whetstone – Madin confirmed that Slack had previously asked to borrow one from him – to sharpen it, and had never meant to use the weapon to murder his mistress.

Slack's aggressive nature was in evidence at the trial itself, where he interrupted witnesses, flew into sudden rages, and leapt to his feet in an attempt to attack George Wilson when the latter claimed that Harold was his son. There was no way he could escape the eventual outcome, and 'wilful murder' was once more the jury's verdict. As sentence was pronounced, Slack appeared to go beserk, ranting and swearing in a shocking manner before being led away, struggling with his guards.

William Edward Slack was hanged on Tuesday 16 July 1907. Shortly before the execution, he wrote a

Brockwell Lane, where Lucy threatened to kill herself at the Donkey Racecourse. Dennis Middleton.

long confession in the form of a letter to the *Derbyshire Times*, in which he set out his version of events. How much of this is true may well be questioned, but one does not have to accept Slack's view of himself as a helpless male snared by a *femme fatale* to suspect that something was almost certainly going on between Lucy and himself. George Wilson said he had never seen Slack before in his life, but Slack had without a doubt worked at the Theatre Royal in 1905, and was seen there by another cleaner, Helen Osborn, on the day of the murder, in conversation with Mrs Wilson, just as he had claimed. On another occasion, Helen had seen Lucy in the Shambles in town with a man who may or may not have been Slack, but who was definitely not her husband.

What William Madin saw on Avondale Road sounded very much like a lover's quarrel, and it is surely significant that Lucy was seen to call Slack back to her two or three times as he tried to leave. Mrs Elizabeth Slack, giving testimony, stated that she knew something had been going on for the last two years, as her husband had often gone out for the night, not telling her where he was visiting, and returning late. She had also heard gossip about his relationship with an unknown woman. Slack in his confession showed a familiarity with the 'penny dreadful' style of literature, but unless he was a very accomplished writer of fiction, the core of his story rings true. His detailed account gives dates, times and places for the events that would have taken a great deal of inventing if untrue, and some at least are substantiated by the testimony of others.

Whatever the rights and wrongs of the case, it had cost both Slack and Lucy Wilson their lives. After this, the third shocking murder to hit Chesterfield in a matter of a year and a half, the town settled down with a sigh of relief. But only for a while.

Highfield Road, Chesterfield, where Slack hacked Lucy Wilson to death with a hatchet in view of witnesses. Dennis Middleton

CHAPTER 16

Murder at the Roadside Inn
1907

The *De Rodes Arms* had long occupied a strategic location at the junction of four roads, not far from the church in the north Derbyshire village of Barlborough, and its licensee was almost as well established. Miles Gosling, although a young man of thirty, came from a respected local family who had lived in Barlborough for several generations, and in the process established themselves as considerable owners of property. His grandfather, who at one time had run the inn himself, had also owned Hollingwood colliery and a successful brickmaking company. Miles's father had also run the colliery for a time before turning to farming, where he and his son had worked together to ensure a prosperous business.

To outsiders, Miles Gosling seemed to have inherited his family's good luck. Married to a well-to-do lady from nearby Worksop, landlord of his own inn, and owner of a hundred-acre farm, his situation must have been envied by many of his neighbours. No wonder he was always so pleasant and

Rose and Crown, *Barlborough, where William Mullinger called prior to his fatal encounter with Miles Gosling.* Dennis Middleton

cheerful, the kind of man most would have chosen as a drinking or sporting companion. What possible worries could trouble him?

All the same, Miles Gosling was troubled. An affable landlord, he was less impressive as a businessman. Accused by one acquaintance of 'indifference towards business', after four years in charge at the *De Rodes Arms*, he found himself in debt. By the standards of the Gosling family the amount owing was small, but in the early twentieth century to admit to being a debtor meant genuine disgrace in the eyes of one's neighbours and friends. Like Joseph Henry Bowman in Mosborough three years before, Gosling was not prepared to endure the stigma of owing money, however little. In all likelihood he had already made plans for a final solution of the problem.

On the morning of Tuesday 5 March 1907 William Mullinger and J W Anable set out from Derby into north Derbyshire, making for Barlborough and the *De Rodes Arms*. They carried a writ from the Sheffield brewers Messrs Whitmarsh, Watson & Company claiming an unpaid bill, which, with costs, totalled £60. The job in hand was to 'levy a distress' on Miles Gosling's goods in lieu of the non-payment. Both men were experienced in this kind of work, Mullinger in particular being a veteran of sixty, and no doubt they regarded this morning's task as the routine serving of a writ.

They were soon to find out otherwise.

Having got as far as Chesterfield, Anable, who had business in the town, stayed for a short while to conclude it. He sent Mullinger on to take possession of the *De Rodes Arms*, promising to follow soon.

The elderly bailiff reached Barlborough around 1 pm, stopping briefly at the *Rose and Crown* before going on to the *De Rodes Arms*. There he informed Gosling of the writ and of his instructions to take over the inn on behalf of the claimants. The landlord appeared to receive the news calmly, and Mullinger left the inn to explore the buildings and livestock to the rear of the premises.

While he was looking the place over, Gosling also left the hostelry and crossed the nearest field, entering a second field where his neighbour John Hibbert was busy ploughing with his team. The landlord asked to borrow Hibbert's shotgun, and the farmer agreed at once. After all, Gosling had often borrowed it before when going on shooting expeditions.

Permission having been granted, the landlord walked to the back of the other farmer's house, and asked Mrs Hibbert for the gun. The weapon was hanging up in its usual position on the kitchen wall, too high for Mrs Hibbert to reach, and she asked Gosling to get it down himself. Gosling took down the double-barrelled shotgun, and as he turned to go back outside told the farmer's wife that he would fix a problem with one of the hammers on the weapon. He then left the house.

Carrying the shotgun under his arm, Miles Gosling made towards the inn. On the way back, he was seen by miner Fred Egglestone, who asked what he was doing. Gosling told him he intended to shoot a cat, and went on for the farm buildings adjoining his public house. William Mullinger was inside the barn, his back to the door as he inspected the interior. He was not expecting Gosling, who appeared behind him and shot the luckless bailiff at point-blank range. The shotgun charge tore into Mullinger's side, blasting out one of his kidneys and leaving a terrible, gaping wound. The stricken man collapsed to the ground.

Gosling then calmly closed the barn door and went back to the *De Rodes Arms*. Leaving the shotgun close to the back wall of his house, and apparently totally unperturbed, he proceeded to serve drinks to his customers inside. As no doubt he knew, anyone who had heard the shot would think it was a sportsman in search of game in the fields nearby. In fact, Hibbert was later to comment that he put it down to Gosling shooting sparrows, something the landlord had been known to do on previous occasions. As he served, Gosling may have looked at the poster on the wall above the bar, advertising a play being performed in the neighbourhood. Its title, *The Murder at the Roadside Inn*, must have seemed grimly appropriate.

Soon afterwards J W Anable arrived at the inn. Surprised not to find Mullinger waiting for him, he asked Gosling if the bailiff had called, to which the landlord replied that he had not seen him. Anable, knowing from experience that his colleague was not one to shirk his duty, and would have followed instructions, was not convinced by the easy answers of the landlord. He told Gosling he would wait until Mullinger arrived, and while doing so would have a look around. Gosling then offered to show Anable the wine cellar, where he assured the officer that he would find 'more than enough to satisfy him'. Wisely, as it turned out, Anable declined, and instead went into the yard, Gosling accompanying him as he walked around the farm buildings.

As they approached the barn, the Sheriff's officer heard a tormented groan from inside. Horrified, Anable exclaimed: 'My God! What was that?' Gosling affected total surprise, but Anable was determined to investigate. Entering the barn, he found the shot bailiff crawling towards the door on hands and knees, with blood pouring from the wound in his side. Mullinger's wound was mortal, and as Anable lifted him in his arms, the stricken man pointed to Gosling, and told his colleague: 'That man's shot me.'

Gosling immediately denied that he was responsible, but by the time Anable lowered the fatally injured Mullinger to the ground and went running for a policeman, the licensee had already disappeared.

Miles Gosling walked through a small gate to the back door of his house, where he picked up the shotgun he had used once

De Rodes Arms, *Barlborough, scene of the shooting of bailiff William Mullinger by landlord Miles Gosling in 1907.* Dennis Middleton

already. Loading the weapon and placing the butt against the ground, he turned the weapon on himself, pressing the trigger with his foot. The blast from the shotgun ripped into his head and neck, tearing away most of the right side of his face. It inflicted hideous injuries that rendered him beyond help. Miles Gosling fell to the ground, and died almost at once.

The second shot had brought several people running to the scene, among them Fred Egglestone and Mrs Gosling, who found her husband just before he died outside the house. Two local medical men, Dr Godwin and Dr Magee, arrived in time to give what little help they could to the dying Mullinger, who was moved to a nearby house and finally succumbed to the six-inch wound in his side two or three hours later. Due to the nature of the wound, he did not suffer severe pain, and was conscious until the end. Barlborough's rector, the Reverend A S Dowling, comforted the dying man and heard his last prayers.

The murder and suicide hit the village of Barlborough like a thunderbolt. No-one there had ever dreamed that the affable, easy-going Miles Gosling, of all people, would prove to be a cold-blooded killer. His financial problems also came as a surprise to them, as the landlord had kept his debts a secret from everyone. Once the evidence was examined, however, there was no possible doubt that he had deliberately killed William Mullinger, and the spare cartridge found in his pocket indicated that Anable would have been next, after which Gosling would presumably have taken his own life. The knowledge that Anable had gone for the police had served only to hurry forward the last act of the tragedy.

As with the Mosborough killings, many came forward afterwards to claim that, had they known what was wrong, they would have been happy to clear the debt. Gosling's family, it was said, could have found the sixty pounds in as many minutes. But, like Joseph Bowman before him, Gosling was too proud to contemplate admitting that he had been foolish enough to get into debt. Instead, he preferred to die, and to kill. By the time his relatives discovered his true situation, they were too late to prevent a real-life murder at the roadside inn.

CHAPTER 17

I Will Put Your Bloody Lights Out
1912

In the early hours of Sunday 19 May 1912, Constable John W Burns was walking his beat in Birdholme, one of the southern districts of Chesterfield. He was not alone. Accompanying him was Alfred Johnson, a thirty-one-year-old married man and the father of six children, who worked as a filler at the Grassmoor colliery. According to later testimony, Johnson had been an admirer of the police force from childhood, and had always tried to assist them whenever possible. He and Burns had been on friendly terms for some time, and the constable described him as 'a friend of the police'. It seems likely that Johnson may well have been employed unofficially as a police informer.

Having made the rounds of the district for two hours and more, the two friends halted on a footpath that led on to Park Street, where the Johnson family lived at No 78. As they were talking, the policeman caught sight of a man coming towards them along the footpath from the direction of Boythorpe. Evidently he had not seen Burns and Johnson. The former checked his watch and saw the time was 1.10 am. When the man came closer, the constable shone his torch into his face,

Park Street, Birdholme, home in 1912 to both killer John Mowbray and his victim Alfred Johnson. Ann Krawszik

and discovered this was someone else he knew. The man in the spotlight was John Mowbray, who lived at No 37 Park Street, on the other side of the road from Johnson. Mowbray had a background of poaching and other minor offences, and had fallen foul of the authorities in the past. At forty-five he was older than Johnson, but had worked with him and his brother at Grassmoor colliery. Dazzled by the light, it is possible that he failed to see or to recognise Johnson; certainly this is what he claimed later on.

From his reaction, it would seem that Mowbray regarded Burns as a personal enemy, who was subjecting him to unfair persecution. According to Burns, the surprised man, who appeared to be the worse for drink, exploded with a torrent of abuse, and in sentences heavily laced with expletives assured the constable that he knew who he was, and told him to put his light out, following up with the threat that he had 'something in the house' that he would fetch, and 'put your bloody lights out!' Burns' version of events was that he told the foul-mouthed Mowbray to go home, and watched him trudge back to No 37.

After talking to Johnson for a few more minutes, the policeman set off back for his own home on Storforth Lane. He had left Park Street and reached Derby Road when he heard what sounded like a gunshot, and made towards it.

Mowbray had indeed returned to No 37, where he lodged with the Lloyd family. Some time during the early hours of Sunday 19 May, Mrs Elizabeth Lloyd heard Mowbray shouting to her husband from the foot of the stairs, urging : 'Bill, come on down, there's two of them!' Mr Lloyd was sleeping off the effects of a hard night's drinking, and his wife told Mowbray to be quiet. He said nothing else to her, but made noises downstairs as if moving things about, and she assumed he was getting himself something to eat for supper.

Soon afterwards, Mrs Lloyd heard another voice calling to Mowbray from outside the house, apparently taunting him and daring him to come out. Mowbray, clearly angered by what Mrs Lloyd described as this 'tantalising', shouted back that if he did come out, the person or persons outside would 'bloody well know about it!' She heard him leave the house, and a noise like someone scrambling over a wall, but did not hear anything more until he returned some minutes later.

Around 1.30 am, Annie Gallimore, who lived next door at No 39, was lying on her living room sofa when she heard Mowbray shout at someone: 'I'll put you to sleep, you bastard!' She then heard him call for Mr Lloyd to come downstairs. Annie dozed off, but was woken by someone banging on the door of No 37. She was on her way up to bed when she heard the gunshot, and on looking out of the bedroom window saw the body of a man lying on the ground in front of the houses. She waited half an hour before venturing out, and discovered to her horror that the body was that of Alfred Johnson, who had been shot dead.

Elizabeth Lloyd heard Mowbray return to the house, and call to her husband again, telling Mr Lloyd that he had 'done it.' Going downstairs, she found Mowbray, in a frightened state, with the hair standing up on the back of his head and looking 'so awful' he scared her too. He gave her a garbled tale that he had been attacked by two men. An old gun belonging to Oswald, her fourteen-year-old son, was on the kitchen table.

Mowbray was still asking to talk to Mr Lloyd, but Elizabeth went to find her neighbour, Mrs Millard. On coming back, she saw Mowbray trying to reload the gun, and Oswald scuffling with him, fighting to snatch it from him. Convinced he was trying to kill himself, mother and son managed to disarm Mowbray, who now ran out of the house.

Meanwhile P C Burns had retraced his steps, worried about his friend. He checked the Johnson house without success. Burns eventually found Johnson's body lying facedown in a pool of blood, a few yards from the 'closet' (outside lavatory) of the Lloyd house on Park Street, and with 'a terrible wound in his side.' Burns took the corpse to the Johnson family home, later accompanying his dead friend to the mortuary. Shortly after 2.25 am he and P C Buggins visited No 37, and took possession of the gun, together with caps, powder and shot. The weapon was not loaded, but had been fired not long before.

John Mowbray sought sanctuary with his mistress, Maud Beeston, who lived with her young child at No 2 Hadfield's Yard. Obviously agitated, he told her he had killed someone, and that he had 'shot the wrong man.' Mowbray repeated a similar story to Maud of an attack by two men. One, the man he had meant to shoot, was Burns; the other, his victim,

Mowbray claimed not to have known. He then fell asleep, to be awoken later by William Lloyd, who with his family and other neighbours had now seen the body of Johnson. Mowbray, with Maud and Mr Lloyd, walked out on to Wheeldon Lane, where the killer was arrested at 4.10 am by Sergeant Birchall, and taken to the police station. On the way, and afterwards in custody he repeated his wish that Burns had been killed instead, and claimed that the policeman had run away.

At the inquest on 28 May, Chesterfield surgeon Dr W J Symes outlined the horrific nature of the fatal wound inflicted on Alfred Johnson. The murder weapon, an old muzzle-loading gun with a shortened barrel and the stock trimmed down, had been used by Oswald Lloyd in his games of soldiers a few years earlier. On this occasion it had been crammed with powder and shot almost to the muzzle, and fired into the victim at point-blank range, scorching his clothing and tearing an enormous hole through his body from left breast to right armpit. The force of the lethal blast had blown out and destroyed the right lung and most of the heart, blackened the right side of the chest and smashed all Johnson's ribs. In the view of the doctor, it would have been possible to pass the entire barrel of the gun through the man's body, by way of the wound that had been made. Ironmonger William Britt, proprietor of a well-known Chesterfield business established in 1818 and which has only in recent years ceased trading from its South Street premises, would later testify that Mowbray had, some time before 19 May, bought powder and shot to the value of 1/9d (8p) from him, telling the shopkeeper he was going to shoot some rabbits.

Also present at the inquest was Herbert Johnson, who identified his murdered brother Alfred. While giving evidence, he informed the inquest jury that he was a good friend of Mowbray, who he had known for nearly twelve years, and that

South Street, Chesterfield, view from Beetwell Street. The former premises of William Britt's ironmongers, with their distinctive ornamented balcony, are shown second from left. Ann Krawszik

they had 'never had a wrong word'. At this remark, the hard-bitten Mowbray broke down and wept.

When it was Mowbray's turn to speak, his story differed markedly from that of P C Burns. He claimed that when he and the two men had met, Burns had twice struck him in the face. He had gone out of the house only after being provoked by the taunting voices, and had taken the gun to frighten, rather than to inflict injury on anyone. Mowbray protested that he did not even know the identity of the man he killed, and fired the gun when startled as Johnson sprang out at him unexpectedly. The inquest jury were disinclined to believe him, and returned a verdict of wilful murder after a mere ten minutes of reflection.

After an appearance before the magistrates, Mowbray went for trial at the Derbyshire Assizes on Tuesday 25 June. Here, as the case unfolded, it became clear that he had a more than

Advertisement for William Britt, ironmonger of South Street. Here Mowbray bought powder and shot for the gun with which he killed Alfred Johnson. T P Wood, Almanac, 1912; Chesterfield Local Studies Library

reasonable argument in his favour. Elizabeth Lloyd could confirm that he had been tormented by 'tantalising' voices outside the house, and Annie Gallimore and another neighbour, Mrs Millard, had heard him shouting to some unseen person that he would put them to sleep. A stone bottle that Alfred Johnson had carried was found near the Lloyds' house, indicating that he might well have been hidden in the outside lavatory, as Mowbray claimed.

The behaviour of Constable Burns also seemed open to question. He appeared evasive when questioned by Mr Hadfield, the Defence Counsel, who was not satisfied with some of his answers. Burns had stated that he removed his helmet and tunic once he found Johnson's body, in order to be less visible to the gun-toting Mowbray, but Hadfield contended that he had done so in order to more easily assault the latter with his fists,

Statues of MPs James Haslam and William Harvey, Miners' Offices, Saltergate. Haslam handed in a petition to save Mowbray from the gallows. Ann Krawszik

perhaps for the second time that night. The Defence Counsel also pointed out that Johnson could not have been the unseen man who taunted Mowbray and then ran away, as he had been shot in the chest at close quarters. Rather, Mr Hadfield suggested, it must have been Burns who called out and then fled once Mowbray came outside with the gun. Mowbray's own accusation that Burns had been there, and had run away 'like a bloody greyhound dog' appeared to have some substance to it, as did his claims of victimisation. On the other hand, he had no bruises to prove that he had been attacked and struck.

The Defence argued for a manslaughter verdict, stating that Mowbray had reacted after provocation and while under the influence of drink. The jury, though, were once again swayed by the Prosecution view, which argued that

Christ Church, Stonegravels. Ann Krawszik
INSET: *Christ Church cemetery, where John Mowbray was buried in 1947.* Ann Krawszik

Mowbray had bought the gun beforehand, had no marks of injury, and had gone out intending to do harm, taking Johnson's life. Mowbray was found guilty of murder, and sentenced to death.

An appeal was promptly launched, and heard on 15 July. Mowbray's defence focused on the fact that he was drunk and therefore not responsible for his actions, but this argument was dismissed together with the appeal.

Site of Mowbray's grave. The stone has since been moved, but that of his son, who predeceased him and is buried beside him, may still be seen. Terry Cocking

The execution date was fixed for 30 July, and it looked like the end for Mowbray, but 14,000 well-wishers petitioned for a reprieve, again citing his drunken state and the possibility of provocation. The petition was presented by James Haslam, the Miners' M P for Chesterfield.

Apparently the Home Secretary was more amenable to these arguments than the Chesterfield and Derby juries and judges had been, for on Wednesday 24 July, less than a week before he was due to hang, it was decided that John Mowbray should be 'respited until further signification of His Majesty's pleasure'. This the *Derbyshire Times* correctly translated as a life sentence, which with good conduct was likely to be reduced to fifteen years' penal servitude. So indeed it proved. Mowbray returned to Chesterfield in 1927, having served his time, and spent his last years as a well-known character in the town. His home was a caravan on Newbold Back Lane, and he found work maintaining and repairing chimneys. According to those who knew him, he also continued his poaching activities, selling slaughtered rabbits to regular customers from his old Model T Ford. He died at a ripe old age exactly twenty years later, in 1947, and is buried at Christ Church cemetery in the Stonegravels district of Chesterfield.

The gun which killed Alfred Johnson was held for many years as a tagged exhibit at Chesterfield Police Station on New Beetwell Street, vanishing mysteriously just prior to the building's demolition. As to its present whereabouts, there remains – as with the murder charge brought against its former owner – a more than reasonable doubt.

CHAPTER 18

I Never Saw Such a Sight
1912

Times could not have been much harder for Mary Churchill. The year 1912 saw her and her family struggling in the grip of utter poverty, unable to find enough money to feed themselves. A young woman of thirty-four, Mary had already borne seven children, two of whom – Katie and Edward – were physically handicapped to the extent that they were unable to walk. Providing for such a large family was an unrelenting task, made worse by the fact that Mary's husband Edward, currently a market-man at Grassmoor colliery, had not been able to find regular work. Now, to add to their burden, four of the children had fallen victim to whooping cough, in 1912 a potentially fatal illness that meant doctor's bills at best, and perhaps something far worse.

Worn down by the daily battle to feed her children, Mary's own health had begun to suffer. Grown gaunt and haggard from lack of nourishment, she had for some time complained of terrible pains in her head, and was subject to violent trembling fits. Edward Churchill had been worried about her, but in July 1912 seems to have felt that his wife was beginning to recover. He had managed to secure work at Grassmoor colliery, and when he left their home at No 9 Angel Yard for the pit at 5.30 on the morning of Friday 12 July he noticed nothing untoward in her behaviour. To be sure, there was no food in the house, and when Mary presented her husband with his 'snap' she told him it would be his last, as she had only one dry crust left over, but perhaps he did not regard this as unusual in their poverty-stricken household. He was to be proved terribly wrong within the next half-hour.

The sleeping arrangements for the sizeable Churchill family normally meant that Mrs Churchill slept in one upstairs room with the baby and two-year-old Edward, while nine-year-old

Julia shared a bed in the next room with her younger sister Katie, the remaining children using the attic as their bedroom.

Around 6 o'clock that morning Julia awoke to find her mother bending over her, one hand gripping the girl's shoulder while the other held an open razor. Glancing sideways to the other children in the bed, Julia saw that Katie was bleeding from a deep gash in the throat.

According to the young girl, Mary Churchill then asked her: 'Shall I do them all?' Acting instinctively, but with great courage, Julia laid her hand on the razor, and felt her mother release her hold on it. Getting out of bed, the child ran out of the room and upstairs to the attic, taking the razor with her.

Mrs Churchill, evidently thinking she had gone downstairs, went down in search of her. In the attic, Julia showed the razor to her eleven-year old brother John and told him what had happened. She hid the bloodstained weapon under a pillow. Soon afterwards she heard her mother coming back up the stairs, calling out and asking her daughter for the razor. Julia replied that she had not got it, and did not know where it was, and after a while Mrs Churchill went away again.

Meanwhile young John Churchill, terrified by what he had heard and seen, ran out of the house to the next door neighbours, the Owens family, and hammered frantically on the door. Henry Owens, who worked as a valve fitter at the Bryan Donkin factory, heard the noise and answered the door. It was now about 6.10 am. On looking out, he was surprised to see Mary Churchill standing beside her son, one arm around his neck, a wild expression on her face as she patted him gently on the head. Owens found it hard to make sense of Johnny's gabbled story, but heard something about cutting children's throats. The ominous silence of Mary Churchill also disturbed him.

Another neighbour, Mrs Jane Barton of 11 Angel Yard, had been up at 6 am and was in the yard preparing to shovel out the ashes when she heard a woman's voice crying out: 'Oh dear! Oh dear!' Going further up the yard, she saw Johnny and Mary Churchill talking to Henry Owens, and went to investigate. It was plain to Mrs Barton that the boy was scared, and like Owens she made out that he was trying to describe an attack of some kind on the children. She asked Johnny if there

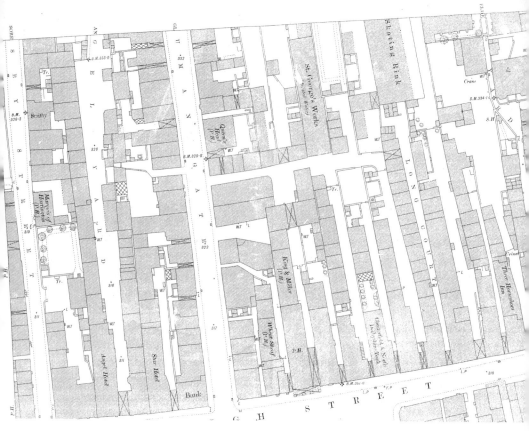

Map showing Angel Yard in the centre of Chesterfield, where Mary Churchill killed three of her children with her husband's razor. Ordnance Survey Sheet XXV.6.9, edition of 1878, Scale 1:500. Reproduced from the 1878 Ordnance Survey map. Chesterfield Local Studies Library

was any blood, and on being told there was became frightened herself, asking Owens to go and look, as she was too afraid. She stayed behind with Mrs Churchill, who was now sitting on Owens' doorstep.

Still in his stockinged feet, Henry Owens went into the house and upstairs. He found baby Annie breathing her last, and two-year-old Edward covered with blood. In the next room was his four-year-old sister Katie, her clothes and the bed saturated with blood from a throat wound. Owens came down the stairs two and three at a time, shouting to Mrs Barton to fetch a doctor, and a third neighbour, Mrs Margaret Kelly, ran off to find Dr Chase.

Just before Owens reappeared, Mary Churchill told Mrs Barton that she did not know why she had done it, but 'something came across my head'. She added that she had thrown the razor away. When her neighbour asked her again for the reason, Mrs Churchill, trembling and clearly overwrought, answered that she did not know. Summoning up her courage, and leaving Henry Owens to keep an eye on Mary Churchill, Jane Barton made the journey to No 9 Angel Yard and up the stairs.

What she saw there horrified her, and she was later to remark that: 'I never saw such a sight.' Annie, the baby, lay at the top of the bed, and young Edward at the bottom, both with cuts in their throats. The bed and the room were spattered with blood.

P C Weavill, on his beat in the vicinity, heard the commotion and attended the scene at 6.15 am. He saw Edward and the baby with their throats cut, and went outside to question Mary Churchill. Gathering from her replies that she was responsible, Weavill placed her under arrest and took her to the station, returning to the house. This time he found Katie, also with a severe wound in her throat. Searching the house, Weavill found an envelope with handwriting on it on the washstand in the front bedroom.

By now Dr R G Chase had been summoned, and examined the three victims. Baby Annie was already dead, and Chase could barely find a pulse with Edward. He rushed back to the surgery for dressings and breathing apparatus. On his return he was met by Julia, who handed him the razor which she had hidden under the pillow in the attic. Chase made a postmortem examination of Annie, and found that the baby had died from a deep two-inch wound on the right side of the neck. Edward and Katie, suffering similar wounds – the boy's jugular vein was completely severed – were taken to hospital still living, but both children died later that day.

Mary Churchill was imprisoned at Derby Gaol, but the next day, Saturday 13 July, Mr Churchill received a telegram from the prison governor telling him his wife was dangerously ill and that he must come at once to Derby. Edward Churchill did so, and found Mary in a very low state, but with medical assistance she recovered enough to appear before the Chesterfield magistrates on Thursday 18 July.

Both here, and at the inquest the previous Friday, evidence was heard from Edward Churchill and his young daughter Julia, both understandably distressed by their experience. The weeping husband recalled that his wife had been good and hard-working, and that they had struggled to survive on his strike and relief money, some 16 shillings a week for the whole family. He spoke of the head pains his wife had suffered, and admitted that there had been insanity in the family; apparently Mary had a half-sister confined at Mickleover Asylum. Julia, who sobbed as she gave her testimony, impressed those present by her courage and the clarity of her evidence. When leaving the stand she was embraced and comforted by Reverend Father Faulkner, who as priest to the Roman Catholic Churchills had undertaken to care for the bereaved children. That Mary Churchill had killed three of them was all too clear, and she was remanded to the next Assizes on a charge of wilful murder.

The message that she had written on the envelope was read out in court. A heart-breaking farewell to her husband and family, it told Edward Churchill that his wife regarded herself as a burden to him, and hoped that God would forgive her for what she had done. Mary urged him to look after the children, and hoped that they would pray for their mother. Cuts or scratches found on her throat at the time of her arrest indicated that she had made a futile attempt to kill herself.

When at last she appeared at the Autumn Assizes, she did so as the patient of Dr Charles A Greaves, the Medical Officer of Derby Gaol. By now Mary Churchill was a pitiful reminder of the woman who had seen her husband off to work a few months before. At thirty-four, she looked old and care-worn, huddled in a chair with a grey shawl covering her shoulders and her hat tugged low over her eyes.

She was allowed to attend only under Dr Greaves' supervision, and it was soon clear that she was unfit to plead to the murder charge. Certified insane, the wretched woman was confined to an asylum, to be detained there 'during His Majesty's pleasure.'

Mary Churchill had killed out of love. Caring for her children, forced constantly to watch the privations they endured as the family struggled on the brink of starvation, the ordeal had proved too much for her fragile mind. Finally, it had given way in an act of murderous violence towards those she loved most. In the end, incarcerated as a madwoman, shut away from the world, perhaps she paid the most terrible price of all. It comes as a shocking end to this most tragic of stories.

CHAPTER 19

A Killer in the Kitchen
1924

Most people in Staveley knew the Lowton family, who for several years had operated as small-scale entrepreneurs in this mining village to the north-east of Chesterfield. At one time Mr Lowton and his sons had themselves run a footrill colliery at Norbriggs, one of several distinct districts in the large and widely dispersed Staveley parish, but this had proved unsuccessful and was eventually closed down. Altogether a more going concern was the tripe dressing business run from a stall by his wife, Mrs Adelaide Lowton, who for some years was assisted by their son Arthur. It seems that he was expected to inherit the business, but at some point Mrs Lowton changed her mind, awarding the concession to his brother Harry.

By the year 1924 Mr Lowton had died, and the extended Lowton family were living in Wateringbury Grove in the Lowgates area of Staveley. A quiet street of terraced houses, it opened on to the main Lowgates Road, and was closed off at its far end, rendering it more secluded than some neighbouring streets. Adelaide Lowton, now a widow of sixty-eight, lived at No 29 with six other members of the family. These were her son Ernest, Arthur and his wife Hannah, and their three young

Lowgates district of Staveley, where the Lowton family lived at Wateringbury Grove. Dennis Middleton

children. Ernest, a single man in his forties, was something of
an invalid. He suffered from heart problems which had caused
him to give up his job as a collier, and had for a time worked as
an insurance agent. Arthur, who at twenty-seven was
considerably younger, still worked as a miner. His twenty-five-
year-old wife Hannah was also a local girl who came from
Woodthorpe, another of the Staveley districts. The couple and
their children had been living at No 29 for about a year. The
third son, Harry, lived next door with his family.

Arthur was an easygoing, happy-go-lucky young man who
made friends easily and was well liked by most of those who
knew him. A regular visitor to the Staveley public houses, he
was also known to venture further afield into South Yorkshire,
and to make more than an occasional bet. The trouble was,
that Arthur had grown rather too fond of this carefree lifestyle.
By late 1924 there were signs that he was drinking heavily, and
that the alcohol and gambling were taking over. It was clear
that Arthur did not have enough money to keep up this way of
life. Unfortunately, it was equally evident that he did not mean
to give it up. Seeing this disturbing change in his behaviour,
Adelaide Lowton transferred the inheritance of her tripe
dressing business from Arthur to Harry, a decision which
Arthur almost certainly resented.

Two weeks before Christmas 1924, Arthur Lowton left the
house at Wateringbury Grove, giving no explanation of where
he was going. He did not return until 26 December. During
his absence, Mrs Adelaide Lowton discovered that £46 had
been taken from a box she kept in her bedroom.

When Arthur came back to the house, he remained close-
mouthed about where he had been and what he had been
doing, but it later came to light that he had been on a
gambling and drinking spree in Yorkshire, blowing most of the
stolen money at Rotherham Woodlands and Leeds.
Determined to get to the bottom of the matter, Mrs Lowton
waited until her son was asleep in bed, and searched the
pockets of his clothes. She found that all Arthur had left was
£1-17s-6d (£1-87 p). This she took charge of, saying nothing
to her son but knowing that he would realise what had
happened.

According to Henry Lowton, all the family knew of the theft and the fact that Arthur was responsible, but rather than accuse him directly they were waiting for him to come clean and admit to what he had done. Arthur, it seems, was not the confessing kind. Instead, a far more ruthless solution was already in his mind.

At 9.45 on Saturday night, 27 December 1924, Arthur Lowton walked into the kitchen of No 29, where the other adult members of the family were about to have their supper. Without saying a word, he sat on the sofa, facing Adelaide, Hannah and Ernest Lowton, who were seated opposite. For a while he appeared to sit in silent contemplation, then suddenly reached into his pocket. When his hand reappeared, it grasped a revolver, and he pressed the trigger.

Ernest, who was taking a smoke, was the first to be hit. The bullet struck him in the neck, and he slumped back into his chair, his pipe falling to the floor. Switching aim quickly, Arthur shot at his wife. Hit in the hand and neck by the same bullet, Hannah crashed to the ground in the corner of the room next to the fireplace. Adelaide Lowton tried to get away, and managed to reach the back door, but as she tugged it open, her son fired again. The bullet tore through her back, piercing her right lung, and Mrs Lowton collapsed across the kitchen threshold, killed outright.

Leaving his victims where they lay, Arthur Lowton ran headlong up the stairs to the bedroom where two of the children slept. The third child, fortunately, was staying with Hannah Lowton's parents at Woodthorpe. Amazingly, two-year-old Muriel and six-year-old Ronald were still asleep, not

Woodthorpe district of Staveley, where Arthur Lowton's wife lived before her marriage. Dennis Middleton

having been roused by the gunshots. Once inside the bedroom, their father bolted the door from inside.

Downstairs, Ernest Lowton managed to get out of his chair. Seeing his mother was dead, he went to Hannah, and established that, though badly hurt, she was still alive. He had told her 'God be with us' in an attempt at reassurance when two more shots were heard from upstairs. Thinking that Arthur had killed the children, Ernest struggled outside and next door to his brother Harry's house, where his frantic knocking was answered by his young niece Adeline. Close to collapse, Ernest gasped out his story, and the little girl ran up to the end of the street, hoping to find help.

As it happened she was in luck, for William Bradley was passing the end of Wateringbury Grove on his way home from work at Lowgates. Adeline grabbed his arm and told him: 'He's shot my auntie!' While Bradley was trying make sense of what she said, he caught sight of P C Jarman coming past and called the policeman over.

Once Jarman was told of the situation, the three of them went to No 29. As they entered the passageway or 'gennel' between the houses, Bradley cautioned Jarman to be careful, as a firearm was involved.

Reaching the back door, the two men saw Mrs Lowton lying dead in a pool of blood across the doorstep. Jarman stepped over the body and went inside, Bradley and the girl remaining behind. After a while the constable came out, telling them to stay where they were, and went to find further assistance. No doubt thoroughly frightened, young Adeline went back to her parents' house.

Bradley could hear moans coming from the downstairs room, and was unable to bear the noise. He entered, and found Hannah Lowton crouching in a corner, her face covered with blood, while Ernest, who had evidently returned to No 29, was seated in a chair. Bradley did not realise that he was hurt, and got him to bring water and a clean cloth to wipe the blood from Hannah's face. She was still moaning and weeping for her children, thinking them dead, while Ernest murmured sadly: 'My poor old brother.' Bradley asked where the killer was, and when Ernest replied that Arthur was upstairs, he pushed the sofa and a sewing machine against the staircase door to prevent him coming out.

After what to him seemed an age Jarman returned, with a doctor and several more police officers. They found blood splashed everywhere about the kitchen, where bread stood on the table ready to be cut for supper, and Mrs Lowton's blood-stained spectacles lying by her body. Told by Jarman that he could go, Bradley now departed. On reaching his house, he found that blood still coated his hands from where he had helped clean Hannah's face.

Hearing no sound from upstairs, the police decided it was time to move. Two officers removed the obstacles from the door and ascended the stairs, while another two found a ladder and placed it against the wall to the front bedroom window. Both sets of policemen proceeded with caution, knowing they had a gunman to deal with. A dummy policeman was raised to the window to draw any possible fire, and when no shots came, a genuine officer ventured to look inside. He saw Arthur Lowton crouching on the bed, between his two young children. He appeared to be glancing quickly from one side to the other, as if awaiting their next move.

Not sure whether or not he was still a danger, the officer smashed a pane of glass, but Lowton did not respond. At a given signal, the officer leapt into the room at the same time as the two on the stairs burst in through the door. Seizing him, they found that he was barely conscious, with blood pouring from wounds in the head and chest. Ronald Lowton had crawled to the bottom of the bed, but Muriel, who was close to her father, was soaked with his blood. Thankfully, both children were otherwise unharmed. The murder weapon, a five-chambered Remington revolver, was found beside Lowton, all five chambers having been emptied. Four extra bullets were found in his waistcoat pocket.

Having secured their helpless prisoner, the police handed him and the other living victims over to Dr Tonks of Staveley, who had them conveyed to Chesterfield Royal Hospital in the Staveley Company's ambulance. Adelaide Lowton was removed to the Staveley mortuary, and later to Chesterfield mortuary where a post-mortem examination was made.

At the inquest on Tuesday 30 December, Henry Lowton identified the body of his mother. He also confirmed that eighteen months earlier Mrs Lowton had turned over the tripe dressing business to Arthur on condition that he acted as proprietor. This apparently had not worked, as Arthur had always been drinking and taking money from the business. As a result, his mother had transferred it to Henry instead. Arthur had then left the stall to work on the pit bank at Ireland colliery. The coroner informed his jury that it was hoped all three victims would recover, but that Arthur Lowton would not be fit to appear.

At the Chesterfield Royal Hospital, staff battled to save the murderer and his victims. Hannah Lowton had sustained two wounds, one to her thumb as she raised a hand to protect herself, the other to her neck below and behind the angle of the jaw. Ernest Lowton, who had lost a great deal of blood from his neck wound, had been in a semi-conscious state when taken to the hospital. Arthur Lowton had shot himself in the chest and then through the right temple, the bullet going through his right eyeball and lodging forward of the brain. Both bullets were still in his body and head. The excruciating pain of being shot through the eye had caused the rapid movements of his head observed by the police officer at the window.

This time, luck was with the victims rather than their attacker. Hannah and Ernest Lowton did indeed eventually recover from their wounds, although no doubt they and the youngsters carried deeper psychological scars. Arthur Lowton, who had done his best to kill them all, was not so fortunate. He died of septic meningitis caused by his head wound, on Saturday 3 January 1925, exactly a week after his attempt at multiple murder.

Wateringbury Grove, Staveley where Arthur Lowton shot and killed his mother Adelaide, and wounded other members of the family in 1924. Dennis Middleton

CHAPTER 20

Death on the Farm
1925

Ｏne of the last of the collieries to be established in Derbyshire was Shirebrook, where sinking operations began in 1896. Formerly a small farming village on the far eastern side of the county and close to the Nottinghamshire border, Shirebrook's population increased tenfold within its first five years, the quiet rural retreat transformed to a 'Wild West'-style boom town well supplied with 'saloon'-type public houses where miners and navvies – some living in huts or tents along the railway embankment behind the market centre – brawled in the streets, and a five-man police force often battled to keep order. Life in the 'Wild East' of Shirebrook was sometimes hazardous in those early decades. In 1923 a pitched battle took place between a poaching gang and law officers in nearby Scarcliffe Wood. A decade earlier, police had been chased out of a house in Station Road by two poachers firing shotguns at the fleeing officers!

Ironically, the most violent and dramatic incident of the 1920s took place, not in Shirebrook itself, but just outside it. Situated in pleasant countryside midway between Shirebrook and the beauty spot of Pleasley Vale, Littlewood Farm was

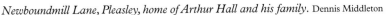

Newboundmill Lane, Pleasley, home of Arthur Hall and his family. Dennis Middleton

only a short distance from Stuffynwood Hall, home of
Shirebrook's long-dead squire Joseph Paget. Its idyllic setting
made it the last place one would think of as a venue for
murder. All the same, it was here in this rustic paradise, rather
than the wide-open mining town, that two brutal slayings were
to be witnessed.

Arthur Hall was seventeen years old, and had worked at
Littlewood Farm as a farm labourer for its owner, Samuel
Bower, ever since he had left school. Bower had until recently
also employed Arthur's father, the Halls living in a disused
First World War Army hut near to the farm. Mr Hall later
moved to work on another farm, and the family set up house
on Newboundmill Lane in Pleasley.

Arthur's father Herbert was later to describe Mr Bower as
'the best man who ever lived', and was sure his son could have
had no complaints over his treatment as a worker. Bower
seemed to have a good working relationship with the young
man, and the two were believed to be on the best of terms. For
whatever reason, this understanding was due to change.

Early in 1925 a young girl called Doreen Lewis was
employed by the Bowers as a general servant at Littlewood
Farm. Aged sixteen, she was a year younger than Arthur Hall,
and the one point on which everyone agreed afterwards was
that he was attracted by her, and made his intentions clear.
What kind of response he received remains open to question.
The authorised version, heard at a time when neither he nor
Samuel Bower were able to put their side of the case, was that
Doreen refused his request that she 'keep company' with him,
and told him she wanted nothing to do with him. Arthur, it
seems, was not easily put off, and having convinced himself
that he was in love with her, continued to pester her. The
tension in their relationship was observed by the Bowers, and
some time in May 1925 Arthur Hall was informed by Samuel
Bower that he was not to sleep overnight at the farm any
longer. By this time he had sent Doreen a threatening note,
handed to her by another worker on the farm, indicating that
he would kill her if she still refused him. He seemed to leave
his work at the farm in good spirits on Saturday 6 June, but
Doreen Lewis may have taken the threat seriously, as she did
not leave the farm on the Sunday.

The idyllic landscape of Pleasley Vale, an unlikely setting for the passion and murder of 1925. Dennis Middleton

That same Sunday, 7 June 1925, Arthur Hall finished his tea at the family home in Pleasley, and set off for Warsop Park Farm, which was run by Mr G H Scott for the Shirebrook Colliery Company. Finding Mr Scott was out, he told the bailiff's wife that Mr Bower had sent him to borrow Scott's shotgun, as he needed to shoot two dogs that had been worrying his sheep. Having no reason to disbelieve him, Mrs Scott gave him the double-barrelled weapon and four cartridges. It would be just enough for what Arthur had in mind.

He set off for Littlewood Farm, loading the gun on the way. When he reached Littlewood at 5.45 pm, he did not go into the farm house, but halted near the Dutch barn by the back door of the house, and called out to Bower's young daughter, Monica, who was playing outside, to 'tell her dad' he wanted him. The child entered the house, and soon afterwards Samuel Bower came to the back door. No-one seems to have heard the ensuing conversation between them, but Bower certainly realised that Hall was in an angry mood, and retreated into the wash-house next to the house itself. Monica saw what was happening and ran in, shouting to her mother that 'Arthur Hall is shooting my Dadda!'

Mrs Bower ran outside, only for the young man to aim the shotgun in her direction. She quickly ducked for cover behind a low stone wall, and Arthur did not attempt to fire at her. Samuel Bower, evidently worried about the safety of his wife, ventured forward and peered out from the wash-house. It was a fatal mistake.

Arthur immediately levelled the weapon on him and fired with deadly effect. Looking up from behind the wall, Mrs Bower saw her stricken husband topple forward, falling into the yard. As she rushed to help him, she caught sight of Arthur Hall aiming the gun at his own head. Unable to look, she turned away as the shotgun fired.

In fact, Hall's first effort at suicide was unsuccessful. The shotgun blast blew off his cap, which was later found holed in two places. Hall dashed round the far side of the Dutch barn, reloaded the weapon, and once more pressed the trigger. This time the charge struck him in the head, and he was killed instantly.

Dr Dennis Perry, called from his home in Shirebrook at around 6 pm, attended the scene. He found Samuel Bower lying prone outside the wash-house, not quite unconscious but barely alive, with a large gaping wound in the right side of his face. The shotgun blast had blown away his cheek and chin, the charges lodging in his head and possibly penetrating the skull. He was rushed to Mansfield Hospital, where he died two hours later at 8.45 pm. Arthur Hall, lying by the Dutch barn, was already beyond help, half his head blown off by the final, self-directed gunshot.

Ruins of Littlewood Farm, Pleasley Vale, scene of the murder of Samuel Bower and the suicide of his killer Arthur Hall. Dennis Middleton

Shirebrook Inspector John Turner and Sgt Marriott were already at the farm, and were able to confirm that Hall must have shot his employer before killing himself. Turner also recovered other items from Arthur Hall's pockets, which were later shown in evidence.

At the coroner's inquest at the *Station Hotel* in Shirebrook, Dr A Green presided as the jury heard testimony from several witnesses. Wilfred Hillsley stated that, at Hall's request, he had passed a note from him to Doreen Lewis, who had asked Hillsley to read it to her. It contained the ominous threat: 'would you like an ounce of lead or six inches of cold knife?' Incredibly, in spite of this blood-curdling, if childish, utterance by Hall, and other verbal threats made in his hearing that he would 'do her in', Hillsley still maintained that he did not think Hall was upset about the girl. In his opinion, the young man was angry because on Saturday he had tried to enlist in the Army although only seventeen, but his father had intervened. Arthur was likely to have been in trouble with the authorities for lying about his age, and this and his father's interference were, in Hillsley's view, the real cause for both violent deaths. Neither he, nor the boy's father, Herbert Hall, had noticed anything out of the ordinary about Arthur prior to the killing.

A similar reticence appears to have obtained among other witnesses at the inquest. Even allowing for the understandably traumatised state of Mrs Bower and Doreen Lewis, there are certain inconsistencies in their version of events. When asked if Arthur seemed attached to her, the young girl claimed not to know. This appears at odds with her later remark that her father disapproved of the attentions Arthur was paying her, and that she therefore told him not to speak to her any more. Doreen again claimed to be unaware whether this rebuff annoyed Arthur or not, and denied that he had threatened to shoot her, although she did admit to his writing letters to her. She confirmed that she had received the letter mentioned by Hillsley, which was destroyed after she had shown it to Hillsley and Mr Bower's two sons, and agreed as to its threatening wording. She did not take the threat seriously, however, and insisted that she had not remained at the farm on Sunday due to fear of Hall. She had not complained to Samuel Bower about him, and the farmer had not told her anything about his reason for wanting Hall to sleep away from the farm.

Poor Mrs Mary Bower, who had been first to witness the terrible injuries to her husband, responded similarly to questioning. She claimed she knew of no quarrel between Hall and Samuel Bower, although admitting that the young man was fond of Doreen. That something must have been going on appears evident from her comment that her husband 'knew I did not like it', and that this was the reason Hall was told to sleep away from the farm, although once again she had not said anything to him about it. She backed up Doreen's testimony that she was not interested in Hall's attentions, and wanted nothing to do with him.

Harder evidence was produced by Inspector John Turner, who found a razor and three separate pieces of paper in the dead youth's pockets. One missive announced that Hall left everything to his mother, while the paper accompanying the razor stated grimly: 'this is meant for Bower'. The final missive was addressed to Doreen Lewis, and was described by Hall

Station Hotel *(now* Shire Hotel*)*, *Shirebrook, scene of the inquest on Samuel Bower and Arthur Hall following the shootings at Littlewood Farm.* Dennis Middleton

himself as 'a few lines of farewell'. Twice referring to the girl as 'my dear Doreen', Hall had written: 'I told you you would get me into a temper, but never mind, if I had got a gun I should have killed five people.' Having delivered this disturbing comment, he had added: 'You will get a better fellow than me.' From these finds, it has to be concluded that Arthur Hall set out with the intention of killing Samuel Bower, and that he did not expect to return alive. The inquest jury duly returned a verdict of murder and suicide, making no comment on Hall's mental state at the time.

The shocking events were obvious enough, but mystery still lingers over their cause. Having threatened to kill Doreen Lewis, why did Arthur Hall instead direct his hatred at Samuel Bower, the man who had apparently been like a second father to him? This murderous attitude is in marked contrast to his last letter to the girl, where his endearments and assurance she will find someone better seem to suggest a closer understanding than Doreen would have had the jury believe. Granted, Hall may have been deluding himself altogether, but it is just possible his passion may have been returned, and that it was this that led to his expulsion from the farm. Doreen, after all, had her job to think of. Somehow, one cannot help feeling that, for whatever reason, the whole story was never told.

Then again, Doreen Lewis may well not have been the only factor in the murderer's thinking. Arthur Hall, it is claimed, had been rejected by her, but he had also been shown the door by Samuel Bower, a man he had come to look upon as a surrogate father. This must have been an equally severe rejection for him, and was further compounded by his actual father thwarting his attempt to join the Army while still under-age. Seemingly let down by everyone he had known and trusted, and with the threat of two years in prison for lying about his age, he had turned his hate and frustration on the father-figure of Samuel Bower, and afterwards on himself. The result was a double tragedy in the farmyard that Sunday evening.

Long since uninhabited, Littlewood Farm is now no more than a set of derelict ruins. All the same, there are some still living who can recall the terrible events that took place there on Sunday 7 June 1925.

CHAPTER 21

A Firewatcher's Fate
1941

Up until 1941, the life of Thomas James Bown had not exactly been crammed with dramatic incident. A married man, he lived with his wife Sarah Elizabeth at No 55 St Augustine's Avenue, on a quiet semi-suburban housing estate in the Birdholme area of southern Chesterfield, and for twenty-five years he had worked as the caretaker at Messrs Eyre and Sons' furniture store in the centre of town. A friendly, inoffensive man, he was well-known in Chesterfield, not least at the *Phoenix* public house on St Mary's Gate where he called in on a regular basis at lunch-times, but this appeared to be as exciting as it was likely to get for him. To most of his friends and acquaintances, Tommy Bown was the last man they would have seen as being marked out for a violent death.

If Bown had one noticeable fault, it was his inability to keep a secret. Whenever anything out of the ordinary happened to him, he seemed compelled to tell everyone about it. On Sunday 30 March 1941, this failing was to have lethal consequences.

In early 1941, the Second World War was running very much in favour of Germany and her allies. El Alamein was a year into the future, and the United States and Russia had yet to enter the conflict. With the retreat from Dunkirk and the terrible bombing of Sheffield in December 1940 still recent memories, Chesterfield was on the alert for further air raids. Many of her inhabitants doubled as fire-watchers when their daytime work was finished, usually sleeping upstairs on the premises. It was true of library staff at the

Furniture store of Messrs Eyre and Sons, on the corner of Stephenson Place with Holywell Street. Here, in an upstairs room, Ernest Prince killed Thomas Bown with a fireman's axe.
Dennis Middleton

Stephenson Memorial Hall. Five minutes walk away from the Hall, Eyre's imposing furniture store dominated the corner of Holywell Street and Stephenson Place. There, Thomas Bown was also carrying out fire-watching duties.

On that fateful Sunday, Bown was daytime caretaker and fire-watcher, on duty from 8 am to 6.30 pm. He had been at the store for three hours when Harry Oswald Eyre knocked to be let in at 11.30 am, and admitted this senior member of the firm. Mr Eyre went up on to the roof, scanning the sky for aircraft, a hobby of his. His was the first of three visits that morning. Shortly after midday the firm's electrician, William Kenneth Bower, dropped in to check a bus timetable in the counting office. Bower stayed for only ten minutes, but before he left he saw Mrs Elizabeth Bown arrive with her husband's lunch. She, too, left soon afterwards.

Apart from the long hours, Thomas Bown's day was not likely to be too arduous, and involved him in routine patrols of the building and checking that all was as it should be. He could not have waited long at the store after his wife's departure. Around 1 pm he was in his usual seat at the *Phoenix*, and it was here that he disclosed his latest piece of news. Bown's mother-in-law had died recently, and as a result he had collected a substantial amount of insurance money. Dorothy Green, the landlord's wife, recalled that he had told her all about it the week before, and that when he visited the inn again on Sunday he showed her a purse that had been left him, which contained four or five pound notes. As always, Bown was very talkative, and letting everybody 'know his business'. His friend Richard Dunks, who dropped in at the *Phoenix* later that lunch-time, found Thomas Bown there already, with a group of companions who included Harry Coupland.

Dunks didn't see or hear anything about a purse, but remembered that Bown bought everyone a round of drinks with a half-crown he produced with a flourish from his pocket. When the pub closed, Dunks and Bown stood chatting outside until about 2.20 pm, then Dunks caught a bus home to Spital, while Bown walked off in the direction of the parish church and presumably on to Eyre's store. It was the last time Dunks saw his friend alive.

Later that afternoon, at 2.30, Harry Eyre came back and was admitted by Bown. He told the caretaker/fire-watcher to expect his son Clive Eyre calling at the store later on, and to let him in. Mr Eyre then went upstairs to his office, changed into his eye-catching plane-spotter's outfit of red sweater, red-and-white checked scarf, green beret and raincoat, and returned to the roof. He was up there until 5.15 pm. Clive Eyre did indeed turn up at 4 o'clock, but although he knocked no-one came to let him in. Going out on the road, he saw his father on the roof, but failed to attract his attention. Clive stayed for twenty-five minutes, trying his best to get in. He couldn't get anyone to answer the door, but was sure he heard someone walking about inside. After nearly half an hour of futile knocking, he gave up and went home.

By 5.15 pm Harry Eyre had come down from the roof , collected some papers from the office and changed back into his regular clothes. He called out to Bown that he was ready to leave, and asked the caretaker to let him out, but received no answer. Puzzled, Mr Eyre explored the building, looking for his employee. His search led him upstairs to where part of the showroom had been curtained off with three beds prepared as a sleeping area for the firewatchers. Peering inside he saw a large splash of red on one of the walls. Entering the makeshift bedroom, he made a horrible discovery. Thomas Bown lay motionless on a bed, his body covered by a blanket except for one foot and one hand, which hung limply down. Drawing down the blanket, Harry Eyre saw a bloody gash in the caretaker's throat. Blood from the wound soaked the bedding, and spattered the walls and floor.

Stephenson Memorial Hall, Corporation Street, where library staff watched for fires only a short distance from the murder scene in 1941.
Ann Krawszik

Harry Eyre rushed to a telephone and alerted the police, and Constables Maynard and Newbold arrived with an ambulance and a member of the AFC. Admitted by Mr Eyre, they were shown the body of the caretaker.

Newbold thought that Bown might still be alive, and he was taken to the Chesterfield Hospital, while Maynard and Mr Eyre made a search of the store. They found no evidence of a break-in, and no money or valuables appeared to be missing from the strong-room. As they could find no weapon, and saw no obvious signs of a struggle, their conclusion was that Bown had tried to commit suicide by cutting his own throat.

At Chesterfield Royal Hospital at 6.15 pm Dr Lewis Gordon Cruikshank, resident medical officer, made a cursory examination of the body, which was partly covered by a blanket, and confirmed that Thomas Bown was indeed dead. In his view, death could have taken place up to three hours earlier. P C Maynard called in to check with him on the cause of death, and Cruikshank agreed with his conclusion of suicide. With regard to the implement he had used, the doctor suggested a sharp cutting instrument, a razor blade or scalpel, which he presumed was embedded deep in the wound at the back of the throat. Cruikshank noticed another wound on the forehead, but thought it could have been the result of a fall. He was asked to make a more detailed examination, but this was not construed as being urgent, and Bown's corpse was not given a post-mortem until twenty-four hours later on Tuesday morning.

Following a more intense search supervised by Detective Inspector Nixey of the Chesterfield C I D it was discovered that a number of items had been taken from the store. The purse that Thomas Bown had carried with up to five pounds in money was gone, as was a bunch of keys including a safe key. Also missing were an electric torch and a fireman's axe. This last item was fifteen inches long, marked 'Chillington Carfax' on the head, and had an insulated handle tested to 20,000 volts. It was further noted that some of the blood on the wall of the room had been smeared, as if wiped by an arm or sleeve.

By now it was clear the police had a murder case on their hands. Acting on information received, they made an arrest on Wednesday 30 April, when Ernest Prince was taken into custody. Prince, a thirty-two-year-old miner and a married man, lived only a short distance from Bown, he and his wife lodging with the Singleton family at No 22 St Augustine's

Road. He had been seen in the *Phoenix* at the same time that Bown had been there, telling the regulars of his good fortune and showing his money. Unlike Bown, Prince was desperately short of funds. He was behind with his rent to the Singletons, and owed money to several creditors in Chesterfield. In fact, he was carrying a list of those to whom he owed money at the time of his arrest. A few days before the killing, he had applied for help to the Public Assistance Board, having no financial means of his own.

According to Mr Singleton, Prince had set off from home on Sunday afternoon claiming he was going to collect money he was owed from Glapwell colliery, a claim that his landlord Mr Singleton knew to be untrue, as Prince had not worked there since 28 January and was due for no payment. When Prince left he had a shilling and a handful of coppers with him, but since then had suddenly seemed to be flush with cash, and was an obvious suspect. His arrest was announced during the Coroner's inquest, which was taking place that same day, and he appeared before the Chesterfield magistrates on Thursday 1 May on a charge of wilful murder.

Evidence was heard from a large number of witnesses, including Harry Eyre, the police, and medical experts. Most telling was that of Dr James M Webster, Director of the West Midlands Forensic Science Laboratory in Birmingham, whose post-mortem study of the body at Chesterfield Royal Hospital corrected the earlier misunderstandings made by Dr Cruikshank in his shorter examination on the day of the killing. Webster would later testify that he had found a sharp,

St Augustine's Avenue, home of fire-watcher and murder victim Thomas Bown.
Ann Krawszik

incised wound to either temple, as well as at least four wounds to the throat. All had been made by a sharp instrument, used with great violence in what appeared to be a frenzied attack. Death was due to skull fracture, laceration of the brain, haemorrhage and shock. A bruise on Bown's left jaw was probably the first blow struck, and marks on his hands indicated that he had struggled against his attacker. He was likely to have been standing or sitting when he received the blow that bruised his jaw, but the head wounds were inflicted while he lay down, and the throat wounds probably after he was unconscious. Another medical expert, Dr H S Holden, reported that a sample of Bown's blood and a smear of blood taken from the jacket that Prince had worn on the day of the killing, were both Blood Group 'O'.

There was no question that Thomas Bown had been brutally killed, and robbery appeared to be the motive. Prince was remanded in custody. Taken to Leicester Prison, he appeared before Mr Justice Oliver at the Derbyshire Assizes on Friday 20 June to face the charge of murdering Thomas Bown.

In his statement, and under questioning, Prince admitted to having met Bown after leaving the *Phoenix*, and presumably after Richard Dunks had caught his bus home. He claimed that Bown, who he had met before but knew only as 'Tommy', had caught up with him on Church Way and invited him into the store 'to have a look around.' He admitted to killing the caretaker, but denied the charge of murder. He also admitted to taking the purse with Bown's money, giving £2 to 'Eileen' and keeping the other £3. He had burned the purse, hidden the bunch of keys under a footbridge near Hyde's Works, while the fireman's axe had been hidden under a pile of debris in the waste at Glapwell colliery when he returned to work. The torch had been dismantled and crushed, and hidden in a drain. Both keys and torch were recovered, but the axe was not.

According to Prince, he and Bown had at first gone into an office around 2.30 pm, but on hearing a knock Bown had gone to answer the door, switching off the light and locking the office door as he did so. This tallied with Harry Eyre's appearance, when he told Bown to expect Clive Eyre's later arrival. Coming back, Bown unlocked the office and switched on the light, and Prince decided he needed to use a lavatory.

Bown told him there was one in the store, and showed him to it. While he was inside, Prince claimed that Bown committed an indecent act.

He then took Prince through to see the 'firemen's corner' in the showroom, and as they sat together on one of the beds Bown showed him one of the three fire axes in the room, studying the insulated handle with its 'tested to 20,000 volts' inscription. Laying the axe on the bed, Bown put his arm around Prince, saying he had always liked him, and made further indecent remarks, resuming his unwanted advances. Prince tried to leave, but Bown grabbed at him and picked up the axe, lunging at him with it. Prince claimed to have sustained a slight graze on the corner of the eye from the axe, but no trace of this remained when he was arrested. A struggle ensued, during which Prince said he didn't know what happened, but which ended with Bown lying dead on the bed. He then took the axe, the purse and the other items, let himself out of the shop, and went through the churchyard to Vicar Lane to catch a bus home. This would have been about 4.30 pm. He denied robbery, claiming he did not know Bown had money on him, and only realized the purse held notes once he got outside. When he saw it, he took it 'to cover himself'.

In defence of Prince, Mr Norman Winning submitted that his client had acted under great provocation, and in self-defence, presenting his attack on Bown as that of 'a decent man who was highly indignant.' As far as the Prosecution was concerned, Prince was anything but decent. In sore need of funds himself, he had seen Bown showing his money around at the *Phoenix*, and latched on to him when he left the pub. With or without provocation, he had launched a savage, murderous attack on the older man, killing him with the point of the fireman's axe. He had then robbed his victim and left, attempting to hide the evidence.

For the Prosecution, Mr P E Sandlands also made the point that Prince had made no plea of self-defence in his original statement, and this was the first time it had been put forward.

On Saturday 21 June, the jury convicted Ernest Prince of wilful murder. Asked if he had anything to say, Prince shook his head. Mr Justice Oliver, passing sentence, told him that he had been convicted by the jury, and that 'it is a verdict with which I concur.' Prince, described as 'calm and resolute' in

St Augustine's Road, where Ernest Prince lived a matter of yards from his victim Thomas Bown. Ann Krawszik

court, was taken back to Leicester, where he was visited by his mother, sister and brother.

Messrs Mather & Co, his solicitors, began work on preparing an appeal. They received an early setback when this was at first dismissed. An execution date was set for 10 July, but this was postponed for another hearing.

On 28 July Ernest Prince appeared before the Court of Criminal Appeal, where Lord Chief Justice Tucker and Mr Justice Asquith ruled that the murder conviction was unsound, due to misdirection by Mr Justice Oliver and the circumstances of the case. They pointed out that, while the jury at the Assizes may not have believed Prince's story, that was not the same thing as disproving it. A reasonable doubt obviously remained, and was enough to invalidate a murder charge. The former charge was quashed, Prince was instead convicted of manslaughter and sentenced to fifteen years' penal servitude.

Sunday 30 March had certainly been a bad day for Thomas Bown. If he was guilty of the indecent advances claimed by Prince, and even if he had attacked him, he still deserved better than the vicious and sustained assault where blows from the fireman's axe were apparently rained on him as he lay unconscious. If Prince's story was untrue, then Bown was doubly unfortunate, being not only brutally killed but robbed of both his money and his good name, labelled as a pervert by the man who struck him down.

At the end of the appeal hearing, it was reported that Prince 'smiled at the decision of the court and strode quickly from the dock.'

Whether his story was true or not, it would seem that he had good reason to smile.

CHAPTER 22

A Man in Black
1960–65

The noise was so loud that it sounded like 'a small explosion.' It roused Fred Clarke from sleep at about 3.20 am on Sunday 12 June 1960, and he hurried to the window to look outside. There he saw a little bubble-car lying on its side in front of his home at No 138 Park Road, a few yards from a lamp-post. Evidently it had just crashed. Mr Clarke ran downstairs and out to the car, but found no-one inside the vehicle. He was struck by how quiet everything was after the crash, with no sign or sound of anyone. He called on his neighbour Leonard Robinson, who had already phoned the police, and two officers were quickly on the scene.

Examination of the ivory-coloured Isetta car, registration 488 KNU, revealed that it had crashed with both lights and engine switched off. A later examination concluded from the empty petrol tank that it had probably travelled down the steep slope of Park Road under its own momentum.

Inside, the officers found bloodstains on the upholstery of the head lining and driving seat. They also discovered two raincoats, one of which – a Burberry-style mackintosh – was stained with blood, and a pair of laced-up shoes by the foot pedals. Glucose barley mints were scattered inside the vehicle, and a tin of tuna and a bottle of vinegar were were also found. A pair of spectacles and a lower set of dentures lay outside, and had evidently fallen on to the road when the bubble-car crashed. A search was made of adjoining gardens

Park Road, where one night in 1960 William Elliott's Isetta bubble-car was abandoned by his killer. Ann Krawszik.

and the Queen's Park Annexe, which was bounded by Park Road on its eastern side, but no trace was found of the driver.

Nine hours later, at 12.45 pm, Roland England was cycling along Clod Hall Lane near Baslow when, at a point 200 yards from the Baslow-Sheffield junction of the busy road, he saw something at the verge of the road against the wall. Taking a closer look, he realized he was viewing the body of a man. England cycled to the nearest telephone box and called the police. Sergeant G J Venables of Baslow responded to the call, and he and England returned to the body, which lay facedown, one arm outstretched above its head, the other wedged against the wall.

Dr S M Evans, summoned to the scene, established that the man was dead, but full examination was left to Home Office pathologist Dr David Ernest Price, who arrived to view the body at Clod Hall Lane and afterwards made a more thorough post-mortem at Newholme Road Hospital in Bakewell.

The dead man was clothed, but wore no shoes or overcoat, and his stockinged feet showed that he had not walked anywhere while unshod. Dr Price found a number of severe injuries on the body. Bruises to the arms indicated that the man had been gripped hard, while pressure on the neck suggested attempts to strangle him. Death, however, had been caused by shock and haemorrhage following skull fractures due to injuries to the head and neck. These, Dr Price decided, were inflicted by the victim's head and neck being violently kicked and stamped on. The head bore a stud-mark pattern from the boot or shoe of the killer, and abrasions on the face were consistent with the victim's face having been driven into a tarmac surface with sharp chippings. He had apparently been killed elsewhere before being driven to where he was found on Clod Hall Lane, and some attempt had been made to hide his body from the road. The victim had worn dentures, but only the upper set was found with the body.

Linking the dead man and the crashed bubble car, police soon learned the identity of the victim. He was William Arthur Elliott, a sixty-year-old clerk at a training college in Great Longstone. A bachelor, he lived with his sisters in Haddon Road, Bakewell. A visit to the house by police officers

Queen's Park Annexe, where William Atkinson narrowly survived a vicious attack. Dennis Middleton

established that he had left home during the morning of Saturday 11 June and gone to shop in Chesterfield; the glucose mints and the tin of tuna were items requested by one of his sisters. Since then, Elliott had been seen in the *Spread Eagle* public house on Brewery Street on Saturday night, and the last sighting of him had been by Joseph Henry Hicks, a bus driver for Hulleys of Baslow. Hicks, who knew Elliott only as 'Bill', recalled seeing him walk out of a toilet near the East Midland Bus Station, a building bounded to north and south by Beetwell Street and Markham Road. This had been at 10.10 pm on Saturday, and there had been no sign of the bubble-car. The next time anyone saw William Elliott, he was lying dead on Clod Hall Lane. Soon the police were linking Elliott's death with another vicious assault committed just over a week before.

On Saturday 4 June Ted Winfield, landlord of the *Boythorpe Inn,* had been knocked up after midnight by a badly injured man who had come reeling out of the Queen's Park Annexe and across Boythorpe Road to the pub desperately looking for help. Opening the door to let him in, Winfield saw the man was in a bad way. He appeared to have been kicked in the face, and his jaw was broken. The victim, fifty-one-year-old William Atkinson, was treated in Chesterfield Royal Hospital and later interviewed by police. He claimed to have been attacked and robbed, and stated that before the assault he heard someone call out his name, 'Bill', in a Derbyshire accent. He later remembered his attacker mentioning going back into the Forces the next day, and came up with a useful description, of a slim, dark, six-foot man dressed in a dark suit.

It did not take long for the police to notice similarities between the two attacks. Both victims were called 'Bill', closely resembled each other in appearance, down to wearing the same type of glasses, and both had been seen in the *Spread Eagle* on Saturday night. Also the attack on Atkinson had been made in the Queen's Park Annexe, an area adjoined on the other side by Park Road, where the bubble car had been found. It seemed possible that Atkinson had been mistaken for Elliott when assaulted. Further investigation revealed that both Atkinson and Elliott were known homosexuals who 'cruised' certain parts of Chesterfield in search of a likely pick-up. Atkinson admitted to having met a soldier in the toilets on Markham Road, and that the assault on him had followed a sex act between them in the Queen's Park Annexe. Elliott's sister, Miss Sarah Elliott, later testified that her brother often went out in the evenings and at weekends, taking sandwiches and a drink with him, and did not usually return until late at night. She also remembered that on one occasion he had brought home a young man friend by the name of John.

The first real breakthrough came when Mrs Irene Mitchell, the proprietor of a fish and chip shop on Derby Road, came forward with information. On 12.25 am on Sunday 12 June, she had been closing the shop when a young man approached her, asking if there were any fish and chips left. Told there were not, he asked for a match. When Mrs Mitchell handed him a box of matches, she noticed he had blood on his face, and that the knuckles of one hand were bleeding. She knew the man, Michael Copeland, and told the police that he was a soldier. This news immediately tied in with the assault on Atkinson, Copeland having been on leave at the time, staying with his parents at the family home on St Augustine's Crescent.

Interviewed by the police, Michael Copeland – a dark, slim six-footer with a penchant for dressing in black – claimed he

Clod Hall Lane, Baslow, where the body of William Elliott was found by the side of the road. Dennis Middleton

had been out drinking with a friend, and had been attacked by two 'Teddy boys' on the way home, skinning his knuckles in the ensuing fight. He had then called at the fish shop on Derby Road before going home. It sounded fairly plausible, and the police did not pursue

Boythorpe Inn, Boythorpe Road, where William Atkinson came for help after being attacked in Queen's Park Annexe Dennis Middleton

the matter, but their suspicions were aroused again when Carol Bright, a young girl who had met up with Copeland once or twice in the days following Elliott's murder, told them that while they were out together he had informed her that he had killed a man in Birdholme. He later made fun of this remark, and claimed to have been acting, but to Carol it had not sounded like a joke. Copeland was interviewed again at Chesterfield police station, and his home searched, but nothing was found, and he was allowed to go.

In fact, Michael Copeland, although barely twenty-two years old, was already a veteran in the world of crime. His list of convictions, mainly for house-breaking and theft, went back to his early teens, and he had served terms in approved school and Borstal before joining the Army. On one occasion he had been known to possess a firearm, but as far as was known he had no previous record of violence.

Meanwhile, police continued to plead for information from the public. Over the next two weeks thousands of people were interviewed and scores of statements taken. Anxious not to scare off the 'gay' community, the police stressed that no-one providing voluntary information would be visited at home. In 1960, with the findings of the 1957 Wolfenden

St Augustine's Crescent, at one time home of the Copeland family. Ann Krawszik

Report yet to become the law, homosexuality was regarded as a criminal perversion by many. Men like Elliott and Atkinson were forced to indulge their desires in a furtive, secretive manner. It also made them an easy target for their attackers, who knew their victims would be unlikely to talk to the police, assuming they survived at all.

With no proof to apprehend a killer, William Arthur Elliott was found by the coroner's inquest to have been murdered by a person or persons unknown, and Michael Copeland returned to his barracks at Verden-on-Aller, in Saxony, Germany. It was there that the next savage killing took place.

On 13 November 1960, sixteen-year-old Inge Hoppe and her fifteen-year-old boyfriend Guenther Helmbrecht had been to the cinema together, and afterwards decided they would find some privacy in a hut in the woods not far from the Verden camp. At about 9.45 pm, as they kissed and cuddled in the hut, Inge saw a man come past and peer inside. He walked past and stood near a tree, still watching them. Becoming apprehensive, she persuaded Guenther to leave, but as they came out and walked away, they heard the man following them. Inge tried to pull her boyfriend aside to let the man by, but instead of going past he struck at Guenther's neck with a knife. He fell, and Inge ran to get help.

She found two men who went back with her to where Guenther lay, and brought him out of the woods. Sadly, there was nothing that could be done for the young boy, who had been stabbed twenty-seven times in a vicious, unprovoked attack. Guenther Helmbrecht died of his wounds.

Some time before 10 pm, Michael Copeland limped into the Verden barracks, bleeding heavily from a deep stab wound in his thigh. When questioned about it, he stated in front of several witnesses that he had been attacked by two German civilians. A search was made of the area where he said the fight had taken place, but no evidence of a struggle could be found.

East Midland Bus Station, where William Elliott was sighted shortly before his death. Ann Krawszik

Copeland was interviewed by Captain Hubert Lambert of the Army's Special Investigation Branch, and informed of Helmbrecht's murder that same night. He accused Lambert of trying to blame the killing on him. Once more, no proof was found, and following hospital treatment Copeland was interviewed again by Lambert, who demanded point-blank whether or not he was responsible. Copeland did not answer.

An identification parade was held on 2 December, with Copeland present in the line. Inge Hoppe failed to identify him, but Guenther Marchlewski, a civil servant, had no hesitation in picking Copeland out. He had been in the vicinity that night, and had seen a man resembling Copeland standing by a tree and watching the young couple.

Again, Copeland responded with defiance, saying he had nothing to worry about as the girl had not identified him. Questioned about a flick knife he had owned, which could have inflicted the wounds on Helmbrecht, he at first said he had lost it, then burst out angrily that if they wanted it, they had better find it, and would need to prove that he had done the killing. He was right. The knife was not found, and he was not charged. Following discharge from the Army in January 1961, he left Germany and went back to Chesterfield.

Two months later, on the morning of Wednesday 29 March 1961, another body was discovered on the grass verge of Clod Hall Lane, only a short distance from where William Elliott's corpse had been found the previous year. As if to underline the similarity of the killing, a car – a black vintage Morris Oxford saloon, registration JN 230 – was again found abandoned on Park Road, near to where the bubble-car had been crashed. As with the Isetta, the lights had been switched off, and the interior of the car revealed bloodstained clothing and upholstery.

It was established that the vehicle belonged to the victim, who was

Mansfeldt Road, home of George Stobbs, second murder victim of the 'bubble-car killer'. Dennis Middleton

identified as George Gerald Stobbs, a research chemist with the Trebor sweet factory in Chesterfield. A married man of forty-eight with two young sons at public school, he had moved to Chesterfield from the London end of the

Trebor factory, where Stobbs was working at the time of his murder. Ann Krawszik

business, and he and his wife had been living at No 27 Mansfeldt Road. Examination by Dr David Price, who had attended Elliott's body, confirmed that Stobbs had been killed in almost identical fashion, kicked and beaten to death, suffering severe head injuries including compound fracture of the skull. The *Derbyshire Times* immediately asked the question: 'Has bubble-car killer struck again?'

On 29 March, Frances Adlington found a book which proved to be Stobbs' diary while walking in Gladwyn Wood, south of Holymoorside and in the Wingerworth area. A police search at Stubbing Court, Wingerworth, unearthed further articles which were identified by Mrs Stobbs as having belonged to her husband. The obvious conclusion was that Stobbs must have been murdered near here, then driven to Clod Hall Lane and dumped, as Elliott had been before him.

Presently police enquiries revealed that Stobbs, who had left home that evening on the pretext of going to the office, had in fact been seen in three different Chesterfield pubs later that night. According to the son of the landlord of the *Crown and Cushion*, he had seen Stobbs and Copeland together in the pub between 9 and 9.30 pm. It later transpired that Stobbs was known to be associating with homosexuals in the town.

Michael Copeland was brought in for questioning, but claimed to have been out drinking until midnight at several public houses. He denied any connection with the killing, and nothing could be proved

Stubbing Court, Wingerworth, probable death scene of both Elliott and Stobbs. Dennis Middleton

against him. He was released, but was now put under a fairly obvious form of surveillance which was to continue for the next four or five years. Everywhere Copeland went, he found himself shadowed by police officers who made no effort to conceal themselves, and sometimes made provocative remarks. On two occasions, in May and June 1961, he reacted violently and assaulted the officers. The second offence, where he attacked Sgt Thorneycroft after police were called to the *Crown and Cushion*, earned him four months in jail. When he came out, in September 1961, the police 'shadows' followed him again.

Strangely enough, while his troubles with the police continued, Michael Copeland seems to have formed a closer bond with two senior officers, Inspector Ernest Bradshaw, and Inspector Thomas Peat. In 1961 and later in 1963, according to police witnesses, Copeland took the initiative in seeking interviews with both men, and made a number of remarkably revealing comments.

The first of these took place on 4 May 1961, when Copeland had a private conversation with Inspector Peat in Chesterfield police station, part of the interview being overheard by Sgt Trevor Evans. Apparently Evans heard Copeland refer to the murders of Elliott and Stobbs as 'the vengeance of the Devil', explaining that :'When the Devil tells a killer to use violence he has to use it. When the Devil tells me to use violence, I have to use it.' The sergeant left the room then, but on his return gathered from what Peat said that Copeland had admitted to killing Elliott and Stobbs. As no-one else had heard the admission, and Copeland had not made and signed a formal statement, he could not be detained. Details of this interview were not made public until Copeland's trial in 1965, by which time Evans' testimony could not be corroborated, as Inspector (then Superintendent) Peat had died the previous year.

The second interview was with Inspector Bradshaw, and took place on 27 September 1961, after Copeland's release from prison following his assault on Sgt Thorneycroft. This time Copeland admitted to Bradshaw that he had 'associated with homosexuals', although he denied that he was one himself. Thinking that he might divulge something, Bradshaw arranged to take Copeland and a girl friend, Marie Smith, into the country, to Grasscroft Wood at New Whittington, where the young man might feel more at ease. There Copeland made the astonishing statement that he knew he was a psychopath, and that his personality might lead him to commit murder, but quickly added that he had murdered no-one.

After this interview, a further troubled period followed, with Copeland under surveillance from the police, relapsing into petty crime and doing spells in prison for various offences. On two occasions in 1963 he attempted suicide, but each time recovered. Matters finally came to a head when he telephoned Inspector Bradshaw at home on Sunday 17 November 1963 to arrange another interview, and the two men met at Bradshaw's office that night.

This time Copeland told the inspector that he had killed Elliott, Stobbs and 'the German boy', adding: 'I killed them because it was something I hated.' He then gave detailed descriptions of how he had murdered his two English victims, claiming he met Elliott in the *Three Horseshoes* and was driven by him to Clod Hall Lane. Elliott had wanted to commit an indecent act (apparently oral sex), and Copeland had attacked him, knocking him unconscious and finishing him off with a stone from the wall. After disposing of the body he had driven the Isetta back to Chesterfield, parking it at the bottom of St Augustine's Road while he went to the fish shop, before crashing the vehicle on Park Road. Stobbs he had met at the same public house, and 'knew he was one of them'. He had determined to kill him from then on. Stobbs had driven him to the *Blue Stoops* at Wingerworth, where they bought two bottles of beer which they drank at the end of a lane near Stubbing Court. Stobbs made an indecent suggestion and Copeland had killed him, using a clawhammer he had later thrown away.

Giving hatred of homosexuals as his reason for the two English murders, Copeland explained that he had killed Helmbrecht because the young couple had been making love 'like I have seen my mother do many times', and that he had hated them for it. The wound in his own thigh had been self-inflicted, struck during his frenzied attack on the boy. He was at pains to deny that he was mentally disturbed in any way, and insisted that: 'I knew what I was doing.' At yet another interview with Bradshaw, on 12 December 1963, he told the inspector that he regretted killing Helmbrecht, and that: 'What I did was brutal.' Once again, Copeland made no signed confession, and had to be allowed to leave.

There is something almost Dostoevskian about this series of interviews, with Copeland walking into the police station, making startling revelations and seeming to be on the brink of full confession, only to pull back at the last moment. For whatever reason, he obviously felt the need to talk to someone, and Bradshaw in particular may have fitted the role of father-confessor. Perhaps a desire to confess to the crime was continually opposed by the instinct of self-preservation, and no doubt the temptation to string the police along, paying them back for what he saw as harassment. This tension may account for the rapid changes in his mood, from reflection to angry defiance and back again. There seems, too, to be an ambivalence in his attitude to 'gays'. Like Raskolnikov in *Crime and Punishment*, Copeland seems to suggest he is doing good by murdering his victims, only to relent later on of what he has done. And on at least one occasion, with Atkinson, he allegedly took part in a sex act before launching his attack, something he was unlikely to have been forced into.

By the time of the November and December interviews Copeland was again under arrest, this time for actual bodily harm. Marie Smith, his fiancee, had rejected him in favour of someone else, breaking off the engagement, and an enraged Copeland had pushed the new boyfriend through a shop window. This earned him eighteen months at Leicester prison, where he had already done time that year.

Gladwyn Wood, where Stobbs' diary was found. Dennis Middleton

On 25 March 1964, while in prison at Leicester, Copeland was visited by the civil servant William Allen, and asked to speak to him. He then made a lengthy statement, commenting obliquely that 'if the truth was known, I would be put away for a long time'. He admitted to 'homicidal tendencies' and claimed he had been wrong to judge homosexuals, that 'like me' they needed treatment. What Allen made of all this is anybody's guess, but the police began to feel they had the makings of a case, and on Friday 11 December 1964, they charged Copeland with the three murders.

Once charged, Copeland responded with stubbornness and defiance, refusing to answer the charges before the Chesterfield magistrates. After a number of delays due to the difficulty of co-ordinating evidence from the witnesses in all three cases, he finally came to trial at the Birmingham Assizes on 16 March 1965. Mr Justice Ashworth presided, and Graham Swanwick spoke for the prosecution, while the prisoner was defended by Rudolph Lyons.

The trial went on until Friday 2 April, during which time Copeland's private, revelatory interviews with Peat, Bradshaw and William Allen were all brought to light. Evidence was also heard from Carol Bright, now Mrs Townsend, about Copeland's claim to have killed a man at Birdholme, while Inge Hoppe and Guenther Marchlewski recounted their experiences on the night of the Helmbrecht killing. Captain Lambert, who had since been promoted to Major before leaving the Army, described his interviews with Copeland, and the Army's investigation. He referred to Copeland's apparent dislike of the 11th as a date, on the grounds that his mother had died and two dogs he doted on had been put down, on the 11th. The fact that Elliott had been murdered on the 11th was mentioned as a possible connection.

On 25 March an anonymous letter, dated 29 June 1963, was read, which had been sent to the Chesterfield police in September of that year. Addressing someone called 'Anne', the writer, apparently her husband, claimed to have murdered Elliott and driven off in his bubble car. The handwriting was definitely not Copeland's, and the defence contended that this indicated someone else entirely was responsible for Elliott's

Grasscroft Wood, New Whittington, where Copeland was taken in the hope of obtaining a confession. Dennis Middleton

murder. It does not appear to have made a decisive impression on the prosecution, or indeed the jury.

Mr Lyons, who tried unsuccessfully to prevent his client from being tried on all three counts at one time, argued with some justice that Copeland had been subjected to a sustained programme of harassment, taunting and provocation by the police which he compared with 'ancient Chinese torture.' Copeland himself, dressed in his familiar garb of black shirt and black leather jacket, flatly denied each murder in turn as the question was put. During his marathon total of seventeen hours in the witness box, he ridiculed the idea that he was superstitious over the 11th, dismissing the assertion as a joke, claimed not to have 'associated' with homosexuals, and denied any tendencies of this kind in himself. Instead he stressed his artistic nature, admitting that he had written poetry, sketched and painted, and enjoyed late night walks as a chance to meditate and 'study the constellations'.

Mr Swanwick was probably less than impressed, and reminded the jury that all three murders had taken place within ten months, had certain similarities, and that Copeland had been in the vicinity in each case. When this was put together with his repeated admission to the killings during his interviews with the police officers over the past four years, this surely pointed to his guilt.

After three hours of contemplation, the jury returned with a verdict of guilty, and Mr Justice Ashworth passed the death sentence. Copeland pressed for an appeal, but later withdrew his claim. In any event, unlike William Elliott, George Stobbs and young Guenther Helmbrecht, he was not destined to die. On 12 May 1965 the Home Secretary commuted the death sentence, and Michael Copeland was sentenced to life imprisonment.

CHAPTER 23

A Life Cut Short
1966

Mavis Hudson was fifteen, and growing up fast. Too fast, her mother thought. A child of the Swinging Sixties, Mavis was typical of a younger generation that suddenly found itself independent of its elders, and with money of its own to spend. Although not long out of school at Hasland Hall, she was very much into adult activities. Mavis enjoyed a smoke, frequented pubs and clubs in Chesterfield and Sheffield, and kept up with the latest teenage fashions. Her trim, five foot two inch figure, always sharply dressed, attracted the boys, and Mavis had already had a lot of men friends. There had always been someone calling at the Hudson home at No 68 St Augustine's Avenue to take her out for the evening in his flash car, and Mavis seemed to enjoy the variety. Mrs Irene Hudson, herself a widow, noticed that she never seemed to settle on a regular escort, but kept on happily ringing the changes. The trouble was, she sometimes stayed out all night, and didn't come home at all.

By the autumn of 1966 Mrs Hudson decided she had had enough, and that her daughter needed some serious discipline.

Spa Lane, view west to St. Mary's Gate. Now mainly a carpark, Spa Lane formerly included the old Scarsdale Brewery buildings where the body of Mavis Hudson was found in December 1966. Dennis Middleton

Mavis left St Augustine's Avenue for a foster home in Bolsover. As 1966 drew to a close, she had been there for three months, but her lifestyle did not change overmuch. A fellow lodger was later to state that Mavis was a friendly girl who was well-liked by everyone, but added that she had often gone out at night with different men, most of them older than herself. In spite of the enforced move, she maintained good relations with her mother, and came over to Chesterfield to see her nearly every other day. To Mrs Hudson, it seemed that perhaps things were improving with her daughter. Mavis was studying as a trainee hairdresser at Chesterfield College of Art, and had long-term ambitions to set up her own hairdressing business.

On Monday 26 December 1966, Mavis Hudson visited her mother at No 68, and stayed for tea. Afterwards mother and daughter went to the *Sun Inn* on West Bars, where Mrs Hudson worked as a barmaid. Mavis stayed at the pub until about 8 pm, then left, explaining that she had to be back in at the Bolsover foster home by 9 pm, and had better catch her bus home. When she left the *Sun Inn* she was wearing a light blue coat, a black and white pinafore dress over a black polo-neck sweater, and black fishnet stockings. Her black hair was cut short, with a 'mod' fringe parted in the centre; Mavis had dyed it blonde, but after adverse comments from some of her friends had re-dyed it to its natural black. She carried a large new black handbag and a box of Cadbury's Contrast chocolates. It was the last time Irene Hudson saw her daughter alive.

Where Mavis Hudson went between 8 pm and midnight on Boxing Night may never be known, but it was certainly not back to Bolsover. And once again, she did not come home.

On the afternoon of Tuesday 27 December, two young boys were playing on Spa Lane. Nowadays all but completely taken over by car parks, the lane in 1966 had a handful of houses and shops. Nine-year-old Tony Mee lived at No 11 Spa Lane, and he and his friend were on the lookout for cardboard boxes to build a den. The derelict Scarsdale Brewery premises behind H C Bates' electrical goods shop seemed promising, and the two boys decided to investigate. Peering into the dark, litter-strewn interior, Tony Mee made a shocking discovery, and went running home to tell his father: 'I have found a dead body, Dad.' It was 2.50 pm.

Going back with his son, Mr Eric Mee went inside, where he found the body of a young girl lying on her back, naked from the waist down but for her fishnet stockings. Her underwear lay beside her. Horrified, Mr Mee telephoned for the police. Superintendent P Parkes attended in person, and saw that the victim lay on an old cement sack in a filthy room littered with cardboard boxes and radio parts.

Foul play was suspected, and Home Office pathologist Dr Alan Usher was brought to Chesterfield. He viewed the body at 6.30 pm, and performed a post-mortem later at 8 pm. The doctor established that death was due to asphyxia, caused by pressure on the throat, where bruises clearly showed. In his opinion, the victim had died between 10 pm on Boxing Night and 1 am on Tuesday morning. The police had a murder case on their hands, apparently with a sexual element, although no mention was made of any sexual assault. Robbery was discounted as a motive, as Mavis still carried money in her handbag. Mrs Irene Hudson was informed of events at police headquarters, and taken to the mortuary, where she had the sad task of identifying the body of her daughter. The Spa Lane area was cordoned off, and a full forensic search carried out.

The Regional C I D were brought in, and a full-scale murder hunt set in motion. Ann Rollins, a shorthand typist in the Traffic Department, acted as the model in a reconstruction which used a photograph of Mavis, taken at Bolsover Town End Methodist Church Bazaar in October 1966. Copies of the

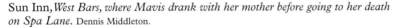

Sun Inn, *West Bars, where Mavis drank with her mother before going to her death on Spa Lane.* Dennis Middleton.

picture were shown onscreen in local cinemas and circulated at dance halls, clubs, and bingo halls on New Year's Eve, where officers questioned those attending. On Tuesday 3 January 1967 the police began a house-to-house check of residences in the area of Spa Lane; on the same day, Mavis Hudson was laid to rest at Boythorpe Cemetery. The next day, Wednesday 4 January, saw the opening of the inquest under Deputy Coroner G A Hotter, where evidence of identification was provided by Mrs Hudson, and brief medical information supplied by Dr Usher.

Meanwhile the police investigation continued. Information was sought from anyone who might be able to help, not least a couple who had been seen parking their car in the lower of the two car parks off Spa Lane around 1 am on 27 December. No doubt for obvious reasons, the unknown couple did not get in touch.

There were, though, several other alleged sightings of Mavis Hudson prior to her death. Two witnesses claimed to have seen her in the *Queen's Head Hotel* on Knifesmithgate between 9.45 and 10.30 pm on Boxing Night. One, a youth who had been a friend of Mavis, stated he had seen her alone, leaning on the juke-box in the old bar. The other witness said that Mavis had been accompanied by a second teenage girl.

For a time it was thought that the other girl might be Susan Morley, another fifteen-year-old missing from home, but soon afterwards Susan was traced in Birmingham, and having questioned her, police were satisfied she had been nowhere near Chesterfield on the night of the murder. By now, though, they had begun to wonder if Mavis had been at the *Queen's Head*, either. Two other witnesses came forward who testified that they had seen her at the Silver Blades Ice Rink in Sheffield at 10.45 on Boxing Night, and this seemed to be backed up by a report received on 10 January that Mavis had been aboard a bus to Sheffield at 8.45 the same night. Two days later the conductress agreed that she had seen Mavis on her bus at 8.30 pm, in the company of several youths.

The response from the public had been good, but unfortunately it provided no breakthrough for the investigators. Enquiries in Sheffield came to a dead end, and the C I D once more focused on the *Sun Inn*, the last place Mavis had been definitely seen alive. It was thought that a young man seen outside the pub at 3 am on the morning of the killing might be able to help, and an identikit picture of him was circulated in the hope of obtaining further information. The police were careful to state that he was not a suspect, merely someone who might have vital information, but once again no breakthrough resulted.

One last witness who claimed to have seen Mavis Hudson alive was sixteen-year-old Shirley Mitchell, of 35 Grasmere Close, Newbold, who had known her 'to say hello to', and was able to recognise her by sight. Shirley remembered seeing Mavis at 9 pm on Boxing Night, coming up from Lordsmill Street and down Vicar Lane to the town centre. Shirley had been standing by St James's Hall on the corner of Vicar Lane where it joined St Mary's Gate, and watched Mavis from across the road as the other girl passed Swale's shop on her way into town. She was quite insistent that it had been Mavis Hudson she saw, and police would later confirm that they believed her story, merely querying the time she gave, which did not tie in with other possible sightings. Regrettably, after a three-month investigation, the police were forced to conclude that their efforts had drawn a blank, and that Mavis Hudson's movements during those fateful hours between 10 pm and 1 am remained a mystery.

When the inquest eventually re-opened on Wednesday 8 March 1967, the verdict itself aroused controversy. Evidence had been heard from Mrs Irene Hudson (now remarried as Mrs Bamford), Shirley Mitchell, Mr Eric Mee, Superintendent Parkes and Dr Usher. Delivering the jury's verdict, the foreman Councillor T Bucknall informed Mr Hotter that he and his fellow jurymen wished it to be recorded as 'death caused by person or persons unknown', and not the customary 'murder by person or persons unknown.' This clearly annoyed the Deputy Coroner, Mr Hotter, who reminded the jury that Dr Usher had provided 'clear evidence' that Mavis's death had been a violent one, and indeed the doctor himself had been quite definite that the marks on the young girl's throat could not have been accidental. Still the jury refused to change their verdict, even when Mr Hotter asked them once again if they wished the word 'murder' to be used, and in spite of his objections theirs was the form of words recorded.

Why did the jury insist on such a verdict? Having heard of Mavis Hudson's lifestyle, did they assume that she had been a willing partner in some kind of sex-game that went badly wrong? Or were they party to privileged information that we can only guess at? Their decision remains one of the final mysteries of the case.

One thing is certain; Irene Hudson had been right. Her daughter had grown up too fast, and it had led to her death. Somewhere, at some time during that cold December night, Mavis Hudson had met someone who would not take no for an answer, and was unlikely to be fobbed off with a box of chocolates. Whether he was a rejected former boyfriend – a bitter youth, or maybe an older married man – or a stranger encountered for the first and last time, during the early hours the situation escalated out of control, and lust became murder. The small, slight girl seems to have been quickly overpowered, with no real signs of a struggle apart from the marks on her throat.

A night out in the Swinging Sixties ended tragically, with a young life cut short in the filth and grime of a derelict building on Spa Lane, and 'death by person or persons unknown' was the final word.

It still is.

Queen's Head Hotel, *Knifesmithgate, where witnesses claimed to have seen Mavis on the night of her murder.* Ann Krawszik.

CHAPTER 24

The Girl with the Elephant Bag 1970

At 11.30 on the morning of Monday 12 October 1970, a young schoolteacher called Barbara Mayo left her flat at No 40 Rockley Road in Hammersmith and made her way to the Hendon intersection of the new M1 motorway, aiming to hitch-hike all the way north to Catterick. Her boyfriend's car had been left in a garage there to undergo repairs, and she had offered to collect the vehicle and drive it back to London. It was something Barbara had done before, and she seems to have regarded it as nothing out of the ordinary. An attractive young woman with high cheek-bones, brown eyes, and a distinctive gap between her top front teeth, she wore her dark brown hair long over her shoulders, and her tall, slim 5 foot 9 inch figure was strikingly garbed in the fashion of the time. She was wearing a three-quarter-length blue barathea coat with tunic collar and eight silver buttons, flared gold and tan brocade slacks, light lilac jersey, sky blue socks and corduroy lace-up shoes. She carried an unusual hand-crafted Nigerian-style handbag in pale tan leather with the image of a red elephant stitched on either side, and fastened with leather thong drawstrings. The bag contained a red leather purse, comb, silk scarf, and some money and paper tissues.

When night fell she had not returned home. The police were alerted by her family and friends, and the next day she was listed as a missing person. The Mayos brought in a private detective to investigate, and Barbara's boyfriend drove up and down the motorway trying to find out if anyone had seen her. By the time six days had passed, her story hit the national press, and shortly afterwards her body was discovered.

On the afternoon of Sunday 18 October the Chomiuk family arrived at Ault Hucknall wood, having travelled by car

Church of St John the Baptist, Ault Hucknall. Buried here is the philosopher Thomas Hobbes, who described human life as 'nasty, brutish and short', and not far away from here Barbara Mayo's life was brutally ended. Dennis Middleton

from Mansfield, intending to pick chestnuts in the wood. They were a large party, consisting of Mr Boris Chomiuk, his wife Helen, grown-up sons George and Ted, Ted's teenage bride Yvonne, and their relative Mr Walter Krzyzanowski. The wood lay only a short distance from the Heath roundabout, now Junction 29 on the M1.

They had only been in the wood a matter of minutes when Mr Krzyzanowski, who had gone on ahead of the others, came running back, obviously upset, shouting that he had found a body. Startled by this unpleasant announcement, the Chomiuks went to look, and found that Mr Krzyzanowski had indeed made a gruesome discovery. The corpse of a young woman, partly covered by leaves and already starting to decompose, lay in the undergrowth. Helen Chomiuk was later to remark that in such a lonely spot, and with winter approaching, it could have lain undiscovered for much longer had their relative not stumbled on it.

Two of the men drove their red 1100 to nearby Hardwick Farm, and told their grim news to farmer's wife Mrs Mary Jeffery. They called the police from the farmhouse, then returned to the wood until the first officers arrived.

When the police reached Ault Hucknall wood, they found the girl's body lying facedown with arms outstretched, partly covered by the blue 'reefer' jacket and a layer of autumn leaves. Although fully clothed, her clothing had been disarranged, and she had been sexually assaulted.

Barbara Mayo's disappearance was already national news, and Scotland Yard detectives entered the investigation at an early stage, arriving at Chesterfield police headquarters on New Beetwell Street in the early hours of Monday morning to set up a murder room. Detective Chief Superintendent Charles Palmer, an experienced officer who had solved many similar cases, assumed command of the operation. A mobile Task Force explored Ault Hucknall wood with tracker dogs, where a caravan was parked as the temporary headquarters for up to thirty officers.

Meanwhile, on Tuesday 20 October, Detective Chief Superintendent Palmer faced the press for the first time. He informed them that the body had been identified as that of Barbara Mayo, and that she had definitely been murdered. Death had been caused by strangulation by a ligature, and she had also been battered about the head. The time and place of

Churchyard at Ault Hucknall. Dennis Middleton.

death remained to be established, and he refused to comment on whether any sexual assault had taken place. He appealed for any information from the public, and from then on the telephone lines were hot with information and apparent sightings of Barbara Mayo before her death.

A murder hunt was launched at national level, with officers checking motorway service areas for the whole 150 miles between Heath and Hendon in an attempt to reconstruct her movements during Monday 12 October. All drivers using this section of the motorway over the three days 12–14 October were appealed to for information. Meanwhile a possible connection was suggested between Barbara Mayo's killing and that of Jacqueline Ansell-Lamb, an eighteen-year-old student teacher, whose body had been found in a wood near Knutsford, Cheshire, further along the motorway. Like Barbara, she had been hitch-hiking north along the motorway. Like Barbara, she had been strangled, and there had been no real attempt to hide the body. Derbyshire and Cheshire police co-operated and exchanged information in the hope of finding the killer.

The inquest on Barbara Mayo took place in Chesterfield on Thursday 22 October, and was conducted by the Coroner, Mr Michael Swanwick. The body was formally identified by Miss Marjorie Mayo, and the victim's address given as 40 Rockley Road, Hammersmith. Mr Swanwick then adjourned the proceedings, pending further police inquiries.

Detective Chief Superintendent Palmer was now running the most full-scale murder investigation seen in Derbyshire up to that time, with hundreds of local officers involved. On Monday 26 October road blocks were set up at all the motorway exits and service stations along the M1 from Heath to Hendon, manned by 1,750 officers, and motorists were asked for information, with the result that thirty possible sightings were reported. The next day, Tuesday 27 October, a man was taken in to Chesterfield police station and questioned for eight hours, but eventually released and eliminated from the inquiries.

Meanwhile posters of Barbara Mayo appeared in post offices and shops and public buildings throughout Derbyshire.

Almost as prominently featured was the distinctive 'elephant bag' she had carried with her from No 40 Rockley Road, which had not been found with the body. Leaflets and copies of the photographs were distributed to the public, while cars fitted with loudspeakers toured Mansfield and Chesterfield appealing for information. Chief Superintendent Palmer was certain that someone must have seen Barbara Mayo at the Heath junction, and guessing that they might have reasons of their own for not coming forward, he promised that any provider of information would remain anonymous 'as far as possible.' It was also his belief that the handbag was probably still in the locality, and might have been picked up by an opportunist who was now afraid to return it.

On Monday 1 November Lindsay Margaret Wallace, a twenty-year-old policewoman from the Stoke and Staffordshire Constabulary, was chosen to act as a 'look-alike' to dress as Barbara Mayo and retrace her journey up the M1 from Hendon, in the hope of sparking someone's memory and obtaining fresh information. Miss Wallace made the long and disturbing trip, stopping at all the garages and service stations en route. Chief Superintendent Palmer was satisfied that useful information was obtained as a result, and this was being investigated with the other leads provided from the earlier motorway 'dragnet' operation. Apparently some officers were sure that the killer must have been a man with knowledge of

Ault Hucknall Woods, where walkers discovered Barbara Mayo's body. Dennis Middleton

the area, but Palmer refused to discount any possibility at this stage. He made the comment that with a sighting of the victim getting into 'a certain make and colour of car at a specific time and place', the case might well be solved.

This remark later proved significant, when on Wednesday 2 December information was received that a girl resembling Barbara Mayo had been seen on 12 October getting into a Morris 1000 estate car on the A610 at Kimberley, in Nottinghamshire, at around 4 pm. The driver was described as a young man of medium height, with mousy hair brushed into a quiff at the front, and probably aged between twenty-five and thirty. The car and its occupants had subsequently driven via Nuthall to Intersection 26 of the M1, and northwards in the direction of Chesterfield. Palmer and his colleagues noted that the A610 provided a cross-country link to the M6, near to which Jacqueline Ansell-Lamb had been murdered. A photofit of the driver was circulated, and the murder squad was strengthened further, with a total of 90 CID and Regional Crime Squad officers working on the case. Chief Superintendent Palmer vowed that: 'If I have to check out every Morris Minor 1000 Traveller in the United Kingdom I will do so, and in fact I have already started.' He also called on the owners of several cars reported as being parked in or near Ault Hucknall wood on 12 October to come forward and assist with the inquiry.

As the motorway checks continued, with over 3,000 drivers questioned in late November 1970, Chesterfield Chief Superintendent Ernest Bradshaw revealed that police still felt there were strong links with the Ansell-Lamb murder in Cheshire, and warned that if they were victims of the same killer, he would almost certainly strike again.

The high-profile investigation continued into the following year, with the murder squad exploring fresh leads, and up to 2,000 Morris 1000 Traveller drivers a week were being stopped and questioned . Wednesday 23 June 1971 saw the arrival of Barbara Mayo's mother and brother in Derbyshire, when they paid visits to the Derbyshire Constabulary headquarters at Butterley Hall, and the Chesterfield murder room on New Beetwell Street. The purpose of their visit was not disclosed by Chief Superintendent Palmer, but was evidently intended to provide further help with the murder inquiry. Unfortunately, it led to no immediate breakthrough in the case, and in spite of all the efforts of the past few months the police seemed no nearer to solving the case.

By this time possible connections were being drawn with the murder of Teresa Bailey in January 1971 (see Chapter 25), and press and public were beginning to express concern that no arrest had been made. When a motorist reported that while travelling on the M1 on Sunday 15 August he had seen a man who appeared to be carrying the body of a young woman over his shoulder in the Pebley area near Barlborough, the police immediately launched a full-scale search of the area. Pebley, a wooded area with fields and ponds, lay only a short motorway drive from where Barbara Mayo had been found in Ault Hucknall woods, and it was possible this sighting might also be connected. On Tuesday and Wednesday 17-18 August police with tracker dogs scoured the woods and fields and the verges of the A618, while frogmen searched Pebley Ponds and another pond at Barlborough Park. Sadly, the search proved fruitless. No body was found, and no definite links made with the Mayo case.

Although Chief Superintendent Palmer was confident that Barbara Mayo's killer would eventually be brought to justice, and made a personal commitment to tracking him down, it became clear that for all the information obtained, nothing had been found which would secure an arrest. As time went on, the Mayo inquiry, one of the most costly murder hunts ever seen in Derbyshire, was scaled down and eventually shelved in favour of other investigations. At the end of 1971 Chief Superintendent Palmer was taken off the case. It must have been a major disappointment to him, as this was the first murder he had failed to solve. He remained determined to find the killer, and when he retired from the force in late 1973 told his colleagues that he intended to continue the search himself. Unfortunately, his efforts failed to track down the murderer.

Twenty-seven years after the death of Barbara Mayo, interest in the case was reawakened when in 1997 Derbyshire

Constabulary re-opened the investigation. A sample of DNA had been found on clothing that Barbara had worn at the time of her death, and with the advent of new forensic techniques, police believed that they might at last be able to crack the case, which it was now suggested could be linked to the Bakewell killing of Wendy Sewell in 1973.

During 1998 many Derbyshire men gave samples of DNA, and were eliminated from inquiries. 9,000 prisoners were also tested, and in early 1999 the investigation widened its scope to Canada, where DNA was requested from a possible suspect. Unfortunately, the hopes of the investigators were once more to be dashed. No breakthrough was made, no hard evidence found, and in 2000 the inquiry was closed for a second time.

It is now thirty-four years since the body of Barbara Mayo was found in Ault Hucknall wood, but no-one has paid the penalty for her death. The killer of the girl with the elephant bag – if still alive – remains at large.

CHAPTER 25

Battered on Beeley Moor
1971

Teresa Joyce Bailey had been struck by tragedy early in life. Born youngest in a family of six children in the east Derbyshire village of Stanfree, she lost her mother at the age of three, and was sent to live with her aunt. The aunt died when Teresa was ten, after which she returned to live with her father, William Copeland, at No 107 Clowne Road. Teresa left school at fifteen to start work, and two years later met local boxer Mick Bailey at the Clowne Gala. There was an immediate attraction, and the couple married at Chesterfield Register Office weeks after the meeting, but the marriage did not work out, and according to her father Mick and Teresa went their separate ways after only a couple of weeks together.

A more lasting relationship was formed when in 1964 she met Harry Martin, a man fourteen years older than herself. By 1971 they had been living together for seven years, and had a young daughter Miriam.

Nine months earlier they had moved from Sheffield to the Chesterfield area. Their present home was a caravan on Hewitt's Caravan Site, on Glasshouse Lane in New Whittington, and both were often seen in the Chesterfield pubs, notably the *Crown and Cushion* on Low Pavement. On the night of Friday 30 April 1971 Teresa Bailey and Harry Martin took the bus from Whittington into Chesterfield, and went into the *Crown and Cushion*. There they separated, Mr Martin watching television in the lounge while Teresa

Clowne Road, Stanfree, where Teresa Bailey lived for a time with her father. Dennis Middleton.

stayed at the bar, talking to a number of her friends. She was still in conversation when Mr Martin left the lounge and checked that she was all right. Assured that she was, he left the pub and walked to the bus stop, assuming that she would meet him there later on.

Teresa Bailey was seen to leave the *Crown and Cushion* at 10.30 pm. She wore a mauve and yellow knee-length psychedelic-style dress topped by a green plastic mackintosh, and blue leather court shoes, and did not carry a handbag. She would normally have caught the bus to New Whittington from the bus stop near the main post office ten minutes later at 10.50 pm. But Teresa did not catch the bus, nor did she return to the caravan site on Glasshouse Lane. By Saturday afternoon Mr Martin began to be worried, and called the police.

Around 3 pm that same afternoon, a family were out rambling on Beeley Moor, an isolated stretch of moorland to the west of Holymoorside, a village close to the western edge of Chesterfield. Suddenly the shocked group stumbled on a body in the bracken. The dead young woman had been savagely battered about the head, and blood was everywhere. The horrified ramblers reported their discovery to the police, and detectives arrived at Beeley Moor in a matter of minutes.

Forensic examination revealed that the victim, subsequently identified as Teresa Bailey, had died from several vicious blows to the head, probably the result of an attack by the fists and feet of her killer when she fell in the bracken. It was thought that the murderer's clothes must have been splashed with blood, and a search was made for any discarded bloodstained clothing.

A murder investigation was launched, with Detective Superintendent Peter Bayliss, Second-in-Command of Derbyshire CID, the officer in charge. As the New Beetwell Street headquarters in Chesterfield was still occupied by the murder squad investigating the then ongoing Mayo case, the new inquiry secured a murder room further up the road, on the ground floor of the former North Derbyshire Water Board HQ.

Attention immediately focused on the 'lost twenty minutes' between Teresa leaving the *Crown and Cushion* and her non-arrival at the bus stop at 10.50 pm. Information was received that a young woman, 5 foot 2 inches tall and with dark shoulder-length hair had been seen talking to her in the Market Place some time between 10.30 and 10.50 pm; this woman, who had spoken to a young man at the Market Place bus stop and an hour later at 11.50 pm, telling him she had been in conversation with Teresa, was asked to contact the Chesterfield Incident Room at once.

Another woman, who rang the Incident Room at 7 pm on Wednesday 5 May, asking to speak to the Superintendent, was also asked to get in touch again. Attempts had been made to set up a meeting with this witness, but due to problems in identifying the location of the rendezvous no contact was made. Aware that several people had been in the pub on the night of 30 April, and must have seen the young woman, Detective Superintendent Bayliss appealed for any of these witnesses to come forward. He pointed out that it would be better for them to contact him than have an embarrassing visit from the police, and warned that if he did not hear from them he would 'ferret them out'. Links were now being drawn not only with the Mayo murder but with the killing of Mavis Hudson in 1966, and a liaison officer was appointed to ensure that both murder squads were kept informed of developments.

Information was sought on anyone absent from home or work during the night of the killing, and as detectives sifted through the data received, they found other witnesses they wished to question. A tall young man had been seen standing at Longside Road in the Beeley area around 11.45 pm on Friday 30 April, a blanket round his shoulders, close to where Teresa's body was found the next day. Further information was requested on this man.

Another possible lead was the woman who had boarded the Kirkstone Road bus at the post office bus stop that same night. She had bought a ticket for Whittington Moor, but then got off the bus before it left town, to meet an unknown man. Anyone on the 10.50 pm bus was asked to get in touch with the police, as it was felt this was crucial to the investigation. In the meantime, police kept the town centre under surveillance in the hope of detaining possible suspects.

On Saturday and Sunday 15–16 May, three undercover policewomen volunteered to join the investigation. They posed

Beeley Moor, where Teresa Bailey was found battered to death in 1971. Dennis Middleton

as members of the public, visiting the town centre pubs, talking to customers and picking up what information they could. Their findings were brought to the Incident Room for further study by the murder squad. Sadly, the efforts of the police were in vain. None of the main witnesses came forward, no suspect was detained, and no arrests made. Eventually, the inquiry was scaled down and the murder squad taken off the case.

In its issue of May 1971, the *Derbyshire Times* commented ruefully on the 'conspiracy of silence' that appeared to be preventing any breakthrough in this, the latest in a terrible sequence of three brutal murders that had taken place in the Chesterfield area in the last four years, all of which remained unsolved. It deplored the fact that, although both Teresa Bailey and Mavis Hudson had been well known to Chesterfield people, none of their acquaintances had come forward with information. Reference was also made to three courting couples seen in cars parked in Ault Hucknall wood at the time of the Barbara Mayo murder, none of whom had broken their silence. Eventually, the Bailey inquiry, like that of Barbara Mayo, was scaled down and closed.

Having encountered tragedy in her childhood and endured a broken marriage, Teresa Bailey seemed at last to have found happiness with her lover and their young child. Unfortunately it was not to be, and on the night of 30 April 1971, aged only twenty-five, she met a terrible and untimely death.

As in the case of Mavis Hudson and Barbara Mayo, her killer has yet to be found.

CHAPTER 26

A Killer's Trail
1977

Young Billy Hughes had a hero; he idolised Johnny Cash. He collected the great Country singer's records, and listened to them every chance he had. Perhaps it is not too hard to see why. The tough, black-clad Cash had himself been a hard man in his time, seeing jail from the inside before visiting Folsom Prison as a reformed character years later for one of his most celebrated concerts. But unlike his unknown young disciple, he had seen the light, and certainly cannot be blamed for the murderous, violent career Hughes chose for himself in years to come.

In August 1976, a pair of teenage lovers were taken by surprise by a mystery attacker in Chesterfield's Queen's Park Annexe. The attack took place in the early hours of morning, the youth being badly beaten up while the young girl was dragged away and brutally raped. Police investigations led to a house on Boythorpe Crescent, across the road from the Annexe, where Billy Hughes was living, and the young man was charged and held for trial for rape and grievous bodily harm.

Boythorpe Crescent, home of Billy Hughes at the time of his arrest for rape and grievous bodily harm on a couple in the Queen's Park Annexe across the road. Dennis Middleton.

Thirty-year-old William Thomas Hughes was already a hardened criminal. Born in 1946, the eldest of six children, his boyhood was spent in Lancashire and Germany, where his soldier father was stationed. From the age of fifteen he had been in trouble with the law, starting off with motorcycle theft and graduating through breaking and entering to assaulting a police officer in Blackpool in 1969. His punishment had followed a similar pattern, from probation, via approved school and Borstal to prison, where he had served a number of sentences. Hughes was later to put his inside knowledge of prison, and of loopholes in the legal process, to deadly use.

Hughes had been a frequent visitor to Chesterfield, and in 1976, although already married, he left his wife Jean to join his new girlfriend, Mrs Teresa O'Doherty, at No 6 Boythorpe Crescent, which was used by the Borough Council to provide emergency accomodation. The couple shared the house with Mrs O'Doherty's sister-in-law Mrs Pat Millan and her husband. They had been there only a fortnight when Billy Hughes was arrested and charged, and Mrs O'Doherty moved out when he made his appearance before the Chesterfield magistrates.

Remanded to Leicester prison, Billy Hughes was due to stand trial at the Chesterfield Court. He managed to delay the trial date several times by apparently changing his mind at the last minute as to which form of trial he wanted. This meant that he was taken nine times from Leicester to Chesterfield and back again, which enabled him to memorise the route in his mind.

In the meantime, due to a delay in the details of the charges being passed to the Leicester authorities, few if any at the prison were aware of Hughes' violent past. Most inmates and warders regarded him as a quiet, well-behaved, fairly ordinary prisoner. They could not have been more wrong. Had they known that this latest addition to the jail was said to have killed two police dogs bare-handed, and that following his arrest for assault in Blackpool he had ripped out the central heating in his cell, they might have been more careful.

As it was, Hughes was allowed to work in the kitchens at Leicester, and at some point managed to steal and hide a seven-and-a-half-inch knife used for boning meat. When his next court appearance came up, on Wednesday 12 January 1977, he was ready to seize his chance.

The day dawned cold and wintry, with a heavy fall of snow. At 8.20 am, Hughes was escorted from the prison by warders Donald Sprintall and Ken Simmonds. As he was classed only as a Category B prisoner, he was given only a cursory 'frisk'-type search by Ken Simmonds, and both warders remained unaware of the stolen knife, whose loss had been reported as early as 3 December. Instead of the police vehicle reserved for the most dangerous inmates on these journeys to court, the party were to be driven to Chesterfield in a taxi with David Reynolds at the wheel, a form of transport permitted for routine court appearances. Sprintall sat beside the driver, while Hughes was manacled to Simmonds in the back seat. While travelling along the M1, Hughes complained that he urgently needed to use a toilet, and Sprintall told the driver to pull in at the Trowell Service area, using the transport side away from the public. Both men accompanied the prisoner to the cubicle, inspected it, and left the door partly open. Hughes was released from the cuffs, used the toilet and came out, to be handcuffed again and taken back to the taxi. It would seem that he used this 'call of nature' to shift the knife to the best position in readiness for attack.

The taxi had reached Junction 29 at Heath, and turned on to the slip road of the A617 that led to Chesterfield, when Billy Hughes struck. The first warning Donald Sprintall had was a sudden, violent blow on the back of his neck. Convinced they had been hit from behind by another vehicle, he clapped his right hand to the place where he had been struck, to find blood pouring from a wound in the back of his neck. Thrown by the suddenness of the attack, Simmonds tried to grab the

Heath Roundabout, Junction 29. Soon after leaving the roundabout for the A617 to Chesterfield, Hughes attacked his guards and staged his escape. Dennis Middleton

prisoner, but Hughes – now armed with the boning knife – lashed out, cutting the warder under the chin and on the thumb. Simmonds made no further resistance, and Hughes jabbed Sprintall in the back, ordering him to put his left hand to join the right behind him. He forced Simmonds to free him from the handcuffs, and manacled the two warders together. On his orders, Sprintall, now weak from loss of blood, climbed into the back beside Simmonds, and Hughes got into the front beside the shocked driver, Reynolds. He took the wallets of both warders and seized their money, also taking money from Reynolds.

Hughes then supervised the driver on what Reynolds remembered as a nightmare journey through Chesterfield and west along the Matlock Road until they passed Slatepit Dale and neared the junction with the narrow country lane leading to Spitewinter. There, on the upward incline approaching Stonedge, Hughes made Reynolds stop the car, and ordered the driver and the two warders out. Sprintall, far gone from blood loss, staggered to the verge and clung to a five-barred gate for support. Helpless to act, all three men heard Hughes swerve and drive away, revving the engine fiercely as he went.

Reynolds and the two injured men were eventually picked up by a passing motorist, and rushed to hospital. There Sprintall underwent an emergency operation on a dangerous neck wound, the knife having plunged in between the spinal cord and jugular vein. He was later told he was lucky to be alive. Simmonds was also hospitalised, but fortunately his wounds were not quite so severe. Meanwhile, Billy Hughes had driven away westward for the more remote, isolated moors.

Later, approaching the village of Beeley, the car went out of control and smashed into a wall. Hughes left the wrecked

Stonedge, the view from Slatepit Dale showing the lane leading to Spitewinter on the left. Here Hughes forced driver and guards out of the taxi and drove off towards Beeley. Dennis Middleton

Beeley village. Not far from here, Billy Hughes crashed his stolen car before taking to the moors. Dennis Middleton

vehicle and made for the open fields in the area of Eastmoor. Here, no doubt, he knew that for the moment he was safe from pursuit.

Scrambling over the snow-covered moors, hammered by an icy, merciless winter wind, he went looking for shelter. A sighting of him near Syda Farm at Upper Loads was later reported to the police. Less than a mile from Syda Farm, he came on the small row of cottages on Baslow Road, Eastmoor, and made for the building known as Pottery Cottage. Forcing his way in, he found an elderly couple there. Seventy-two-year-old Arthur Minton and his seventy-year-old wife Amy were no match for a vicious criminal wielding a bloodstained knife. Hughes was able to subdue them and find out who else was likely to be coming home. He was ready and waiting at 3.15 pm when their married daughter Mrs Gillian Moran came home, to be followed at 3.45 pm by her ten-year-old adopted daughter Sarah and at 6.15 pm by her husband Richard. Hughes overpowered them, keeping each member of the family tied up in a separate room.

Meanwhile the police had been alerted, and a manhunt was set in motion. Tracker dogs and helicopters were used in the hope of running down the escaped knifeman. Unfortunately the weather was gradually getting worse, with thickly falling snow whipped into blizzards by the howling wind and hampering operations. Worse still, the police were to receive information that Hughes intended to return to Lancashire, probably to harm his wife. Following this line of inquiry, the police concentrated their efforts on the area west of Beeley, where Hughes had abandoned the crashed taxi. Unluckily for them, and for others, Billy Hughes had turned east.

At Pottery Cottage, he had already begun to dispose of his victims. Hughes had armed himself with two axes and a knife from the house in addition to the weapon he already carried, and on the day of his arrival at the cottage he murdered Arthur Minton, inflicting multiple stab wounds on the elderly man. Soon afterwards, in a bedroom, he cut the throat of ten-year-old Sarah. He kept up a pretence that they were alive by taking meals to their rooms, but Mrs Moran began to suspect that her father was dead. Mercifully, at this time, she did not know her daughter had also been butchered.

On the morning of Thursday 13 January two council workers, Bob Coles and Ernie Jones, arrived to clean out the septic tank. Mrs Moran came outside, and chatted with them as she signed the worksheet. Neither man noticed anything untoward, but no doubt Gillian Moran was thinking of her family inside the house at Hughes' mercy, and what might happen to them if she did not do as she was told. The workmen completed their task and left, unaware that anything was wrong.

The same day, telephone calls were made from the house by Mrs Moran to Sarah's school, saying she was too ill to attend, and by Mr Moran to Brett Plastics Ltd in Staveley, where he worked as sales director, explaining that he had a cold and wouldn't be coming to the office. Later in the morning, Hughes allowed Mrs Moran to leave the house and drive into Chesterfield alone to buy newspapers and cigarettes. Apparently Billy wanted to see how his escape had been reported; the cigarettes would have been for him too. He

Syda Farm, Upper Loads, where a sighting of Hughes was reported shortly before he made his way to Pottery Cottage. Dennis Middleton

would no doubt have been gratified to read the *Derbyshire Times* report the following day, which revealed that one of three theories held by the police was that Hughes must be holding someone hostage; the others were that he had died of exposure, or had broken out of the police cordon and fled.

At tea-time that day, Hughes decided to visit Chesterfield himself, accompanying Richard and Gillian Moran in one of the family cars. The worsening weather halted them; the party were met by a fierce blizzard and had to turn back.

Undeterred, Hughes waited until the storm died down, then made Mrs Moran drive him to visit a friend across the Nottinghamshire border at Sutton-in-Ashfield. Having covered thirty-two miles, they returned, only for Hughes to order another trip to the same friend's house, ostensibly to pick up some letters. It is difficult to avoid the thought that by now Hughes was supremely confident in his ability to outwit the police, and playing with his captives. Already he must have known that he had little to fear from them.

At 11.30 on Friday morning he allowed both the Morans out to shop in Chesterfield unsupervised. The couple went to five shops and a petrol station in the town, but made no attempt to raise the alarm. As far as they knew, Hughes had at least two hostages alive back at Pottery Cottage. Scared by the number of police officers in town, they got back as fast as they could.

At 5 pm, Hughes made a further trip with the couple to Brett Plastics in Staveley. After a brief chat with the factory supervisor, who asked him about the cold that had kept him off work, Mr Moran went to the office and opened the safe, removing £200 which he handed over to Hughes in the car. Not satisfied with the haul, the killer went back inside with Mr Moran and made a further search, collecting another £100. Considerably richer by now, he directed the couple back to the cottage. Once inside, Richard Moran was tied up and separated from his wife.

Meanwhile, Hughes had been having trouble starting the bronze Chrysler 180 car the Morans owned. At 8 pm that night he sent Gillian Moran to the next door neighbour's house to get help towing the car from outside the cottage on to the main road. Leonard Newman, headmaster of the Carter

Eastmoor, across which Billy Hughes travelled on foot through blizzard conditions to arrive at Pottery Cottage. Dennis Middleton

Lane School in Shirebrook, opened the door to her knocking, and was shocked when at last Mrs Moran told him that the escaped criminal was inside the cottage, that he had Mr Moran tied up, and was now asking for a tow. Mr Newman agreed to get help, and Mrs Moran returned to Pottery Cottage, where an impatient Hughes took her with him to the nearby farm of Bennie Frost, who hauled the Chrysler with his pick-up truck over the treacherous, snow-covered ground on to the road. By then Leonard Newman and his wife had driven to Charles Smart's poultry farm, and from there telephoned the police at Chesterfield.

Back at Pottery Cottage, Mr Frost drove away unsuspecting to his farm. Leaving Mrs Moran in the car, Billy Hughes went back to the house, telling her he needed to collect some road maps. In fact, he was on a more gruesome mission. Bound and helpless, Richard Moran was stabbed repeatedly, bleeding to death from his wounds. His mother-in-law Amy Minton died soon after, her body hacked with blows from the knife and her throat cut as she tried vainly to get away. Despite her bonds and the awful wounds, the poor woman managed to stumble outside to the front garden before collapsing. Hughes covered the corpse with snow, and rejoined the terrified Mrs Moran. The car drove away from what had become a house of death.

When the police arrived at Pottery Cottage, it was to find only the bodies of four murder victims. Once again the hunt for their killer was on. A stream of police cars pursued Hughes and his frightened companion in a high-speed chase north-west through New Mills and Whaley Bridge, until the fugitive was finally cornered in the Cheshire village of Rainow.

Hughes, who had crashed the Chrysler during the pursuit, and switched to a Morris Marina, tried to smash his way through a road-block consisting of a local bus, two police cars and some stiles. He burst through the stiles and ploughed to a halt in a garden, where he was encircled by vehicles and armed police. Holding down Mrs Moran inside the car, he knelt over her, threatening her with an upraised axe, and demanded to be given another getaway car. With police marksmen at the ready and close to the vehicle, Chief Inspector Peter Howse began to negotiate with the killer, trying to calm him down and defuse the situation. The conversation went on for what must have seemed a very long half-hour, and Howse was beginning to think the stand-off might end without violence, when the outside light of a house came on, and Hughes flew into a rage again. Knowing a road block was positioned further along Hughes' escape route, Howse offered him a police car in return for the release of Mrs Moran, who was now hysterical and screaming in terror. Hughes made further demands for shoes (he had left the house barefoot) and cigarettes, which Howse brought and laid on the back seat of the car. The Chief Inspector crouched by the window, trying to keep the killer talking, but Hughes was having none of it, and eventually shouted to him: 'your time is up!'

Realising that he intended to kill his prisoner, and displaying great courage, Howse hurled himself in through the broken window of the car, shielding Mrs Moran with his right arm and grabbing at Hughes. The killer struck at him with the axe, and Howse sustained several painful blows on the arm. It was the signal for the armed police officers, Detective Sergeant Frank Pell and Detective Constable Alan Nichols, to open fire. Pell aimed at the murderer's head from twelve feet away, and as the .38 Smith & Wesson bullet struck, Hughes was heard to shout: 'Oh, bloody hell!' Although hit in the head, he continued to lash out with the axe in a beserk fury, inflicting cuts on both Chief Inspector Howse and Mrs Moran as Pell fired two more shots into him. The marksman must have begun to wonder if Billy Hughes was bullet-proof and unkillable when Nichols fired, and the murderer finally fell dead across a terrified Gillian Moran, dropping the axe. He had taken all four bullets, suffering potentially fatal wounds to the chest, the main artery of the heart, the left side of the skull and the right eye, which had been destroyed by the shot. Mrs Moran, suffering from shock and cuts which fortunately would not prove dangerous, was rushed to hospital in Manchester; for her, fifty-five hours of horror as Hughes' captive was at an end, but a worse trauma – the news that she alone had survived – yet to be realised. The axe-blows inflicted on Chief Inspector Howse caused him to lose the feeling in his right arm for a time, but thankfully he recovered.

Dr Alan Usher, the Home Office pathologist, performed post-mortem examinations on the four victims, and not unexpectedly gave the cause of death as haemorrhage and shock following multiple stab wounds and the cutting of the throats of Mrs Minton and young Sarah. Mrs Moran was not present at the inquest, where Coroner Michael Swanwick's jury returned verdicts of murder for the Mintons and Richard and Sarah Moran, and justifiable homicide in the case of Billy Hughes. They also urged that Chief Inspector Howse be commended for his bravery, and soon afterwards he was promoted to Superintendent and received the Queen's Commendation for gallantry. After the selfless heroism he had shown at Rainow, it was eminently well-deserved.

Shock-waves at the Pottery Cottage massacre spread throughout the country, and in the wake of the violent conclusion at Rainow there were demands for a public inquiry, and answers to any number of awkward questions. Why had Hughes been classed only as Category B, and allowed to work in the kitchens at Leicester? Why had he not been thoroughly searched, when a knife had been reported missing a month before? Why was he transported in a taxi, rather than a police vehicle? Why had the police not searched Pottery

Boythorpe Cemetery, where plans to inter Hughes were thwarted by protesters. Ann Krawszik

Cottage, and the Eastmoor area? Good questions, to be sure, but for Hughes and his victims they came too late.

Even in death, Billy Hughes roused the people of Chesterfield to fury, as plans to bury him at Boythorpe Cemetery sparked a furious backlash from the public. Protesters, many of them women, got into the cemetery before the funeral was due to begin, and clawed at the earth in the pouring rain to fill in the freshly dug grave by hand. The funeral had to be abandoned, and afterwards locals chained and padlocked the cemetery gates. Eventually Michael Swanwick as Coroner gave permission for Hughes to be cremated at Brimington, where again the protesters showed up with placards to express their anger. After the ceremony, on 25 January, Hughes' wife Jean was presented with his ashes; they would not be scattered on the grounds at Brimington.

It is surely a sad irony that only four days earlier, the four victims of Billy Hughes were also cremated at Brimington, where the bereaved Gillian Moran attended the service with 100 mourners. With her husband, daughter and parents dead, she had to begin her life all over again. Unable to live at Pottery Cottage, she sold up and moved away. She was later to remarry, and in 1982, backed by a storm of public outrage, prevented the planned screening of a television play on the murders at the cottage. After the horrors she had suffered, it is hardly surprising she should want to forget the terrible events of those three days in January 1977.

In the twenty-six years since the Pottery Cottage slaughter, there have been other murders in Chesterfield and North Derbyshire, just as there were in the centuries before. It seems a safe bet that in the years to come, there will be more. Sadly, violence appears to be part of our condition, and human nature now – as in previous ages – shows little sign of change.

Brimington Crematorium, where funeral services were performed at different times for Hughes and his victims.
Dennis Middleton

Sources

1. Copies of local newspapers: the *Derbyshire Times*, the *Derbyshire Courier,* and the *Sheffield Star.*
2. Eddleston, John. *Murderous Derbyshire*, 1997.
3. Wood, Thomas Philpot. *T P Wood's Almanac*, 1882–1963.
4. *Reflections* magazine, March 2001.
5. Verbal information from relatives, who have asked to remain anonymous.

Index